MOUNTAIN *Vines,* MOUNTAIN *Wines*

Mountain Vines, Mountain Wines
Exploring the Wineries of the Santa Cruz Mountains
by Casey Young

Published by:
Mountain Vines Publishing, LLC
Post Office Box 922
Santa Cruz, CA 95061 USA

orders@mountainvinespub.com
http://www.mountainvinespub.com

Santa Cruz Mountains AVA map ©2003 Mike Bobbitt & Associates

Cover Design by Richard Curtis   Santa Cruz, CA

Printed in Singapore

ISBN. print ed.   0-9741357-6-3
First printing   2003

Publisher's Cataloging-in-Publication
(Provided by Quality Books, Inc.)

Young, Casey, 1951-
  Mountain vines, mountain wines : exploring the
 wineries of the Santa Cruz Mountains / by Casey Young ;
 photographs by Ken Dawes ; foreword by Charles L. Sullivan. -- 1st ed.
  p. cm.
  Includes bibliographical references.
  LCCN 2003094215
  ISBN 0-9741357-6-3

  1. Wine and wine making--California--Santa Cruz
Mountains. I.Title.

TP557.Y68 2004   663'.2'00979471
        QBI03-200503

*This book is dedicated to the
Latino vineyard workers of the
Santa Cruz Mountains area.*

Acknowledgements

We'd like to acknowledge all of the winery owners, as well as vineyard and winery workers who create that delicious beverage known as wine. Maggie Paul, our intrepid editor, read far into the night to insure that the prose was correct in every aspect. Our friends and children, who patiently waited for us to be done with this book are so very important in our lives.

But we also acknowledge each other, because without our individual contributions and dedication, the book would never have been born.

Contents

Foreword   6

Introduction   9

The Land   10

The History   14

The Wineries   20

    East Side   25

    West Side   58

    Mid-mountains   86

Santa Cruz Mountains
Winegrowers Association   108

Glossary   111

Further Reading   112

Winery Index   113

Foreword

Consumers of California wine are met with a happy, yet complex situation when they meet the term "Santa Cruz" in their quest for vinous satisfaction. Happy they can be in the knowledge that "Santa Cruz" and "wine" are almost invariably related to high quality products from the efforts of an idealistically dedicated band of men and women who are rarely obsessed by the financial bottom line.

The consumer also needs to deal with the complex question of what is meant by "Santa Cruz" in the literature of wine or on a wine label. There is the historic town of that name, the county and the winegrowers' association. But it is the mountains, the Santa Cruz Mountains, that physically define this area of premium winemaking. And it is the Santa Cruz Mountains that give their name to the viticultural district recognized by the U.S. government for its unique character when it designated the region an American Viticultural Area (AVA) in 1981. I'll tweak the potentially confusing nature of the situation by noting there are more Santa Cruz Mountains wine grapes growing in Santa Clara County than in Santa Cruz County. And, of course, San Mateo County is also a small but important part of the AVA.

The authors of *Mountain Vines, Mountain Wines* have correctly, I think, focused on the mountains and their grapes in the title of their book and in their admirably relaxed approach as to who gets to be included.

There are about forty wineries in the AVA and almost all of them operate under the assumption that the production of wine from Santa Cruz Mountains' grapes is a major goal. But most of the product of these wineries comes from grapes grown outside the AVA. Nevertheless, overwhelmingly most of this outside wine comes from AVAs noted for their history of high quality. There is no better example than Ridge's Sonoma Zinfandels. And, of course, there are wineries technically outside the boundaries of the AVA with a powerful historic connection. Bargetto is a perfect example.

The vineyard acreage in the AVA has been growing steadily for forty years, almost doubling since the 1980s. And yet it is considerably smaller than during Prohibition; in fact, it is less than half of what it was in 1900. The reason will become clear as you read through the experiences of the winegrowers here. It is very difficult to grow world class grapes in most of this environment. Powerful corporations are not moved to make the kind of large scale investments here that have marked the recent growth in an area such as the Central Coast. The mightiest of the Santa Cruz Mountains producers are dwarfs compared to the corporate operations that today stand astride much of the California wine industry.

You will perceive a steady *leitmotif* in the goals and attitudes of the men and women who make Santa Cruz Mountains' wine. They are willing to meet the challenge of relative isolation, rugged terrain, shallow soils, cooler weather and coastal fogs for the ultimate payoff: the perceived excellence of their wine. And they do this, for the most part, without the hope of attaining great wealth from their labors.

The history of winegrowing in these mountains is long and lively, dating back to the 1850s. "Mountain Charley" McKiernan raised grapes here while he was fighting off the grizzlies. After the loggers had cleared parts of the land, it was soon found that its soils had a great potential for growing fruit. Grapes were an important crop from these early days. In fact, the intense flavors discovered in Santa Cruz Mountains' grapes made them famous for eating as well as for wine production.

In the early years, focused idealism and self-reliant individualism were as obvious in these mountains as they are today. There were John Stewart of Scotts Valley and Emmett Rixford of Woodside, early champions of Cabernet Sauvignon. Some thought that the Riesling from Dennis Feeley's Lexington Vineyard was the best in the state. There was a French colony of vintners in the hills above Saratoga. Their German counterparts planted vineyards above Los Gatos. In 1890 no less than seventy-six households engaged in viticulture picked up their mail at Wrights Station near the summit of the mountains.

My wife and I came to the Santa Clara Valley in 1958 and were soon living at the foot of the Santa Cruz Mountains. It did not take us long at that early date to discover the beauty of the wines grown in those highlands. By the early sixties the wines of Bargetto, David Bruce, Hallcrest, Mount Eden and Ridge were regular guests at our table. In 1982 the subject of my first book on California wine history focused on the Santa Cruz Mountains and the Santa Clara Valley. I must admit that I am not a neutral observer on the subject matter covered in this book.

When the U.S. Treasury Department held its hearing on the petition to establish the Santa Cruz Mountains AVA in 1981, I was keen to testify in its support. I concluded my testimony by claiming that, "grape for grape, bottle for bottle, the Santa Cruz Mountains district is the finest winegrowing area in the Western Hemisphere." The Treasury official in charge asked for the basis of this claim and I replied with acreage statistics by variety for Santa Cruz County. Virtually every vine in the official state statistics was of a world class variety, such as Cabernet Sauvignon, Pinot noir, or Chardonnay. (Of course, I included Zinfandel in this category.) No other county or district in the New World could make that claim. Napa still had a thousand acres of vines best suited to the conditions of the Central Valley.

Today Santa Cruz has the same degree of varietal excellence, although in recent years other coastal counties have developed a similar purity. But in one respect Santa Cruz Mountains winegrowers still stand out. It is as true today as in years gone by, that no other region has a higher percentage of intensely focused, idealistic men and women raising wine grapes and producing wine.

Charles L. Sullivan
Los Gatos
June, 2003

Introduction

 When we met, Ken and I discovered that we both liked going to local wineries. One day as we sipped a nice Merlot at a Carmel Valley winery, we talked about our other hobbies – photography and writing. Then the light dawned! Why not write about wineries? Better yet, why not produce a book about wineries in our own back yard?

 The research for this book has been enjoyable; we can't say enough about the people we interviewed. They invited us into their homes, climbed over barrels to share their wine and answered our never-ending, and sometimes naïve, questions with patience.

 This is a book about people and wineries. We have deliberately avoided critiquing the wines, believing that our taste may not be to your taste.

 We had to scope this book in order to get it done. New wineries are starting up all the time. With one exception, Clos de la Tech, all the wineries in the book were in the Santa Cruz Mountains Winegrowers Association at the end of April 2003. This leaves out newer wineries such as La Rusticana that hadn't joined the association by that time, as well as local wineries that haven't joined the organization, such as Testarossa. Not all of the wineries we have included are all within the boundaries of the Santa Cruz Mountains American Viticultural Area (AVA).

 We invite you to meet the people and taste the wines of the 50 wineries that are in this book. We're sure you will enjoy them as much as we did.

Casey Young and Ken Dawes

The Land

The French call it *terroir*, an almost untranslatable notion of soil and essence that forms the cauldron of grape creation. Through tradition and legislation, the French have determined where and how particular grape varieties will be grown. This codification is far too restrictive for most Americans, however. For more than a century, Californians have planted vines without too much thought regarding climate or soil. Even recently, with more information at hand, too many viticulturists follow the market rather than the land.

The wine growers and the wine makers of the Santa Cruz Mountains, however, must pay attention to the land or they will not survive. These are small operations, for the most part, an integral part of the mountains and people around them. As you explore this area and talk to the vintners, you will hear again and again that good wine begins in the vineyard.

Before Vineyards

Over 250 million years ago, much of the Santa Cruz Mountains area was under the Pacific Ocean. Waves pounded the edge of the existing North American continent, stripping away the land, leaving steep cliffs. At the bottom of these cliffs, the ocean continued its motion, creating smooth beaches that became marine terraces.

The Pacific Ocean floor churned with energy. The tectonic plates that make up the earth's crust, jostled for position. The two that shaped California were the North American Plate and the Pacific Plate. About 250 million years ago, these plates collided, the Pacific Plate sliding beneath the North American plate, thrusting up over the next 150 years to create the Klamath Mountains in northern California and Peninsular Mountains in southern California. About 30 million years ago, the plates gave up their head-on assault and the Pacific Plate headed north – grinding, sliding and bumping against the North American Plate along the way.

Crumpling the ocean floor, the Pacific Plate pushed up the edge of the North American Plate to form the California Transverse and Coastal Mountains, of which the Santa Cruz Mountains are part. The energy of this collision was so great that it's difficult to differentiate between the sandstone and shale that form these mountains. For a visual of this jumble of rock, visit Devil's Slide on Highway 1 in San Mateo County -- if the road is open, that is.

This collision caused some of the marine terraces to lift from the ocean floor, forming giant steps that climb the mountain foothills. These fertile grounds provide grazing lands and farmland along the Santa Cruz County coast.

Coastal foothills of the Santa Cruz Mountains

San Andreas Fault

Vine growers and wine makers who work in the Santa Cruz Mountains live with the grinding of these two plates on a daily basis. The Pacific Plate containing the Coastal Mountains creeps northward at a rate of about five centimeters a year[1]. Occasionally, it hits a bump. The abrupt leap wreaks havoc on the people and places in and around the Santa Cruz Mountains. Winemakers can find their barrels tossed from one end of the room to another.

The San Andreas Fault, as the convergence between the two plates is called, runs by and through the Santa Cruz Mountains. As you travel around the mountains to visit the different wineries, you'll be driving back and forth across it. To gain an understanding of the geography of this fault, take some time to explore the San Andreas Fault Trail on Page Mill Road.

The last major earthquake in northern California occurred in October, 1989. The Loma Prieta 7.1 magnitude earthquake destroyed huge swaths of downtown Santa Cruz and tossed homes and businesses in the mountains. Like many traumatic events, the earthquake prompted mountain vintners to introspection. Some, like Dexter Ahlgren, got the barrels back on their racks, wiped up the spills and kept going. Others, like Dave and Anne Moulton of Burrell School, redoubled their efforts to create their winery. Jerry O'Brien of Silver Mountain was faced with the decision to rebuild his entire winery or give up. He started again. Others left.

Microclimates

Microclimates are pockets of variation in climate. The microclimate of a vineyard is influenced by nearby bodies of water, altitude and slope of the vineyard, as well as sun, wind, clouds and precipitation. Earthquakes and water etched the folds of the Santa Cruz Mountains, providing multiple variations of hills, mountains, slopes and altitudes. With the San Francisco Bay on one side and the Pacific Ocean and Monterey Bay on the other, climate changes occur just a few feet apart. Even the distance between a winery and Silicon Valley can have an impact on the average temperature of a vineyard.

Vineyards hang on mountain slopes, suspend on ridges and tuck into valleys. They perch at altitudes above 2,000 feet high above the fog line, and hug the valleys at lower elevations. Viticulture in these areas is not easy.

Afternoon fog rolling in

Water

Drive up Highway I-280 on a summer afternoon and you see fog's giant hand slip over the ridge, slither through mountain crevices and cap the peaks. Turn west from the sun-baked Santa Clara Valley and follow a winding road. The fog drip from the trees might slap your windshield. Going over the mountain ridges and down to the ocean shores brings you deeper into the gray. You can almost hear the poet Carl Sandburg's cat feet and you know that the ghostly galleon is waiting in the bay.

The fog is the only moisture in the summer's dry heat. Traveling south from the upper reaches of the Northern Pacific, the California Current dredges up cold water from the lower reaches of the ocean and pushes it to the surface near the coast. Warmer air floats over this channel of cold water, creating fog and pushing it inland, rising 1,500 to 2,000 feet high. While the summer heat can dissipate the fog by eight in the morning, there are times at the coast when only an hour in the middle of the afternoon is fog free.

During other times of the year winter's rain pelts the vines, causing flooding in lower streams and rivers. For example, Cinnabar, perched over Silicon Valley, gets 60 to 90 inches of rain in the winter. After centuries of this type of weather, the topsoil on the mountain ridges is, at most, a foot and a half. In contrast, the sandy loam of the marine terraces can be over four feet in depth.

As dramatic and earth-shaping as stream water can be, vineyards aren't planted by mountain rivers. Under-watered roots search through the shale, rock and clay to reach the aquifer, providing stress to the plant, and adding intensity to the grape's flavor. Where natural water isn't enough, drip irrigation is used.

Slope, Soil, Altitude and Wind

Driving through the mountains produces vineyard surprises. You round a corner to see vine rows staggering up the mountain. Or you wind through towering redwoods on narrow slashes of road, only to emerge in full sun and acres of vineyards.

Two slices of the continent make up the mountains causing the soil and minerals to differ from vineyard to vineyard. East side soil contains limestone, serpentine and Franciscan chert. The topsoil, what there is of it, is clay and sandy loam. On the west side where the land was dredged up from the bottom of the ocean, the earth contains sandstone, the remains of ocean creatures and sedimentary rocks from southern California mountains.

Rocks from Loma Prieta (furthest mountain in the distance)

Of course, there are anomalies due to the close proximity of the sliding plates. Rocks dropped from Loma Prieta Mountain on the east side of the fault crossed the fault line and have since moved twenty-three miles north on the west side of the fault. Limestone close to Ridge Winery was once part of a tropical island. The variation of minerals provides the wines of the mountains with an unexpected complexity.

Most of the areas within the Santa Cruz Mountains don't suffer from the constant high winds that can destroy a vineyard during its growing season, but it does occur. Viticulturists must take care to insure spring winds don't destroy their crops. The ocean and bay provide a consistent breeze that wafts the fog over the mountain crest and cools the hiker, as well as the vineyard worker.

Living Together

Coast Redwood trees, some over 300 feet tall, march up the western side of the mountains, darkening small groves that interrupt grasslands and chaparral. Hiking through these ancient trees creates a sense of timelessness. Scars abound from the excess logging of the nineteenth century – 20 foot wide stumps notched where the loggers stood as they took down the giants. Surrounding the remaining stumps you can find young trees in circles, determined to be there long after we are gone. Sometimes there is no central tree. Who knows what happens when you step into the center of this "fairy ring."

At higher elevations you can see large tracts of trees, small houses perched on impossible cliffs and the occasional vineyard. Yet, stand at the top of Monte Bello Ridge and you see evidence of human encroachment spread out below you in the Santa Clara Valley, as well as the vineyards of Cinnabar and Cooper-Garrod to the south.

As Silicon Valley (San Jose and surrounding regions) has grown, the price of land has doubled and quadrupled in the last decade of the 20th century. The Santa Cruz Mountains' wine business is not very lucrative; a check from the newest millionaire can be tempting.

While some wineries produce wines exclusively from their own grapes, many contract with vineyards in and out of the appellation. Some use grapes from their neighbor's back yards!

Vineyards overlooking Silicon Valley

Winegrowers face mobile co-habiters as well. While the bird bounty is enthralling to the hiker, it's difficult for the winegrower who must protect his or her fledgling berries from a sharp beak. Gophers, the bane of gardeners throughout the region, pop up from under fences in the most annoying way. Fending off deer and the occasional grape-loving coyote is all in a day's work.

Made rugged by adversity, both the winemaker and the wine gain character. This unique combination has created top quality wines for over a century.

(Footnotes)
[1] USGA Web Site (pubs.usgs.gov/publications/text/understanding.html)

The History

The Santa Cruz Mountains have a long and rich history in the wine-making business, going back to the early 1800s when Mission grapes were used to make wine. Today this wine would be considered mediocre by most winemakers and wine drinkers.

For centuries massive tracts of virgin Coast Redwoods covered the mountains. The underground contained substantial lime deposits. The Ohlones lived in and around the mountains. In the mid-1700s Spanish influence began to seep up from southern California and with it a chain of missions. The early monks needed wine to celebrate mass. Among the vines they brought from Spain to their colonies in the New World, they favored the use of Mission vines in California. Franciscan missionaries planted the first of these grapes between 1804 and 1807 in what is now Harvey West Park in Santa Cruz County.

These early travelers heralded the end of serenity in the mountains as the Native Americans and early explorers knew it, but it took another 40 years before the real destruction began. Between 1850 and 1880 18,000,000 board feet of virgin redwood were harvested. The evidence is left behind in places like Big Basin State Park. There, giant redwood stumps bear the notches left by the loggers as they stood on the base of the tree to saw down the timber. While we can look back with sorrow on the natural destruction of a century and half ago, the early loggers and homesteaders were doing what was required to earn a living – a hard living.

Loggers provided another benefit to those entering the mountains for the first time – open land. Granted, farmers needed to clear the stumps, sometimes a daunting task, but the possibility of becoming homesteaders in the mountains became real. Along with fruit and vegetables, many of the immigrants planted grapes for winemaking. During the mid-1800s, initial viticultural plots were established throughout the mountains. Lyman J. Burrell planted near the summit, providing today's Burrell School Vineyard with their historical reference. The Jarvis brothers planted in the Vine Hill district above Scotts Valley; the district that now houses the Santa Cruz Mountain Winery and numerous vineyards, such as Annamaria's Vineyard. The Burns family grew grapes in the Ben Lomond area of Bonny Doon where Jim Beauregard maintains most of the vineyards today. On the eastern slopes, Dr. Robert Tripp established a market in the town of Woodside in 1854, and subsequently made wine and planted grapes in the 1870s. The market, Robert's Market, is still there today and has an outstanding selection of Santa Cruz Mountain wines, as well as wines from many other parts of the world.

By 1875, existing records noted that Santa Cruz had 262,275 vines (about 300 acres) and was making 70,000 gallons of wine a year. However, similar to the situation in the late 1990s, there were more grapes, frequently of inferior quality, than the industry could support. The wine market collapsed, and with it the fortunes of many winemakers within the Santa Cruz Mountains, including the Jarvis brothers who had had the largest holdings.

Undaunted, landowners were planting vines again five years later, establishing many of the areas within the Santa Cruz Mountains that are known for their premium grapes and the wines made from them.

On the east side of the mountains, Emmet H. Rixford planted a small vineyard on the top of a small ridge (cuesta in Spanish) above Woodside. Rixford evokes the type of winemaker that you're more likely to find in the mountains today -- people dedicated to preserving the quality of small vineyards in their wine – versus the bulk winemakers of his own time. The time he spent learning viticulture paid off because his vines are still used by the Woodside Winery today. Cuttings from the vineyard also found their way to Martin Ray, the founder of Mount Eden. Rixford's book, *The Wine Press and the Cellar*, published in 1887, was a staple for new winemakers well into the 20th century.

Further south, another group of winemakers began their ascent up Monte Bello Ridge, home today to the Picchetti, Fellom Ranch and Ridge operations. Vincent and Secundo Picchetti purchased land towards the bottom of the mountain in the early 1870s. The Picchetti family was running their operation well into the 1950s, with people bringing jugs and getting their wine directly from the barrels, similar to today's "Bottle and Cork Days" at Obester Winery.

Further up the mountain, Pierre Klein purchased 160 acres in 1888. Klein was regarded as one of the primary winemakers of his day, winning a gold medal at the Paris Exposition of 1900. His original vineyard, now called Jimsomare, has been replanted with all of the grapes going to Ridge Winery under a 30-year lease arrangement.

Osea Perrone, a dapper San Francisco physician, created his summer retreat, vineyard and winery at the top of Monte Bello Ridge in 1886. The main house, home of summer events and dinners featuring opera stars, forms the core of the Ridge Winery today. Unfortunately, Perrone cared more about his appearance than his health; he died in 1912 from gangrene after refusing an amputation when his leg was damaged in a buggy accident.

14

On the west side of the mountains, John Jarvis reestablished himself with a 36-acre vineyard and winery in 1878. Henry and Nellie Mel established their winery around the same time; Henry Mel went on to become influential in the state wine associations, along with Dr. John A. Stewart, a winemaker in Scotts Valley. These vintners brought in new varieties, expanding the quality and range of Santa Cruz Mountains' grapes. Emil Ernst Meyer, a German florist, completed his 95-acre vineyard, Mare Vista. This was the first vineyard in the mountain to be planted with phylloxera-resistant root stocks grafted with European varietal grapevines. (Phylloxera is a root louse native to the United States that destroyed the European grape vines, but not the resistant American root stocks. It was re-introduced into the U.S. in the late 1850s, destroying large vineyards with European vines in just a few short years.) The Mare Vista operation functioned until 1939.

Henry and Nellie Mel's "Villa Fontenay"

Paul Masson was probably the most notable character to establish a vineyard in the Santa Cruz Mountains in the early 1890s. Born in Burgundy, he immigrated to the United States and began to work with the New Almaden Winery in the Santa Clara Valley which was owned by Charles Lefranc. After Lefranc's death, Masson married Charles' daughter Louise, and went into partnership with Charles' son, Henry. Masson's goal was to make premium sparkling wine using *methode champenois*. A driven man, he created his first champagne in 1892, breaking up the partnership with Henry the same year. However, he was unhappy with the grapes he obtained from New Almaden and ultimately purchased 40 acres in the mountains above Saratoga in 1896. For the next 40 years, he produced champagne – of course, only for "medicinal purposes" during Prohibition. Today, his fine house and land serve as the Mountain Home Winery, a place that produces some wines from estate grapes and serves them during the concerts and events that they hold.

The other significant winery established in the 1880s was the Novitiate in Los Gatos. This winery, established by the Jesuits, lasted until 1985 before closing its doors. The Novitiate was known for its premium wines, and many early Santa Cruz winemakers were associated with the winery in some manner. Today, the winery is used by Mirassou Winery for cellaring and champagne tastings, and is leased by Testarosa Winery for its processing. Many other Santa Cruz winemakers, such as Equinox, also use the facilities.

Things were booming in the wine business as the decade of the 1880s came to a close. Large wineries were built on both sides of the mountains to handle the expanded number of grapes from vineyard owners – large and small. By 1889 the Los Gatos-Saratoga Winery was making 120,000 gallons of wine a year. The Los Gatos Cooperative Winery was making over 300,000 gallons at the same time. On the west side, the Santa Cruz Mountain Wine Company had a capacity of 200,000 gallons.

Associations of grape growers and grape purchasers also began at about this time period. The California Wine Association (CWA) was created in 1894 by six large wine merchants to try to stabilize grape prices and improve the quality of wine labeled "California." The California Wine Makers' Corporation (CWC) was formed shortly thereafter to ensure that the winemakers and growers would be adequately paid for their fruit.

It looked like the California wine industry was poised to take off. However, a number of events, both natural and unnatural, conspired to prevent that from happening. Indeed, the events described below prevented the Santa Cruz Mountains wine industry from recovery for close to one hundred years.

One of the causes of the downslide of the California wineries repeated itself a century later – over planting of vines and subsequent over production of wine. By its nature, this brought down the prices of wine, particularly in the lower end of quality, similar to the $2 bottles of wine available in the early 2000s. The economy in the mid-1890s was also depressed. This combination of events led to disagreements between the CWA and CWC, intensifying through the 1890s as elements of each side maneuvered around agreements that had been made.

A large degree of distrust developed until the CWA brought suit against the CWC in 1897. This started a two-year "wine war." At the end, the CWC was dissolved and the CWA dominated the state wine industry until 1919.

At the turn of the century, most Californian winegrowers planted their vines without any type of grafting – on bare roots. By the end of the 1890s thousands of acres of vines were dying and the growers were confused because the same species produced different capabilities to resist the pest. Phylloxera, carried to Europe on American vines imported for collections, had wiped out many of the French vineyards a few decades before, and had now returned to attack California vineyards that had been planted with European varietal grapevines.

After a great deal of research and exchange of ideas with France, experts determined that the solution was to graft vines onto American rootstocks. The rootstock which was most resistant at the time was the Rupestris St. George, a rootstock which is commonly found over most of the mountains today. Although growers were reluctant to change, Paul Masson's success with the process shifted the technique into common use. Since that time, other rootstocks have been developed that are 100 % resistant to phylloxera.

From the turn of the century until the advent of Prohibition, the wine industry replanted its vineyards and renewed relationships damaged by the wine war. Other than Masson and Rixford, there were few prominent winemakers in the mountains. A few transactions occurred that would influence today's winemaking, however: Giuseppe Locatelli bought a homestead and winery near Eagle Rock in 1898; the Hall family purchased a summer home in Felton in 1891; and Eloi and Pierre Pourroy planted 40 acres of vines above Congress Springs Road in the 1880s.

Photo courtesy of The Museum of Art & History @ The McPherson Center, Santa Cruz, CA

Santa Cruz Mountain Winery/ Ben Lomond Wine Company

With the 1906 earthquake the Pacific plate slipped an incredible 12 feet north along the San Andreas Fault, but the damage was not as profound as that experienced in San Francisco or even provided by the Loma Prieta earthquake of 1989. Paul Masson took advantage of ruined buildings to create a winery in his Saratoga vineyard. Sometime prior to the World War I, another event occurred that would have a significant impact on Santa Cruz winemaking: Martin Ray, the teenage son of a Methodist minister, met Paul Masson. This event didn't bear fruit until after the end of Prohibition.

Prohibition was the looming cloud that finished off most of the premium winemaking in the Santa Cruz Mountains. Paul Masson continued on with his "medicinal" champagne and the Novitiate still made altar wine, but any other winemaking efforts, like much of the nation's liquor production, went underground. During this time, people were allowed to make 200 gallons of wine for home consumption; frequently, more was made. The mountains were well-suited to hiding illegal activities and supplies of bulk wine, usually of inferior quality were transported around and out of the area. Stories of hijackings and break-ins at wineries were plentiful.

The first winery to emerge from Prohibition was run by the Bargetto family. John and Phillip Bargetto opened their place in Soquel in 1933. However, their goal at that time was to produce "jug wines sold in barrels at low prices."[1] In 1941 Chaffee Hall began to plant his vineyards, opening Hallcrest Winery in 1946. In 1945 Dwight Beauregard purchased the Quistorf vineyard in Bonny Doon, land that had originally been part of the Burns holdings.

However, the person who had, and continues to have, the greatest hold on the style and imaginations of Santa Cruz Mountains winemakers was Martin Ray.

Throughout his education and employment as a stockbroker, journalist and real estate broker, Martin Ray remained in contact with Masson. Ray's dream was to own his own vineyard in the mountains. When Masson first began to talk about selling in the 1930s, Ray expressed his interest in purchasing the property. Masson, who did not want to sell to Ray, told him he would be better off buying the undeveloped land to the north of the Masson property – the northern half of Table Mountain. However, after much scheming, with the truth of the transaction shrouded in myths, Martin Ray purchased the property through a third party in 1936.

One of the most significant changes that Ray brought to the wine business was his focus on varietal grapes. Up until this point, most wines had been labeled in the French manner – Burgundy, Chablis, etc. – after regions where the particular grapes were grown according to French law. Wines began to be named for the varietal wine they contained, but there was no guarantee how much of that varietal wine was actually in the wine. Legally, a Cabernet Sauvignon had to contain at least 51% of that varietal wine while the other 49% could be anything else. Martin Ray fought his entire life to increase the percentage of the varietal wine in a bottle named with that variety.

Paul Masson died in 1940 and his former winery died a year later, destroyed by fire in 1941. Close to ruin, Ray refused to sell, instead taking on debt and doing most of the work himself to rebuild his dream. However, once the dream was rebuilt, he was drained. When Seagram's came calling in 1943, Ray decided to sell and move his operation to the north.

Winery workers in the Santa Cruz Mountains.   Photo courtesy of The Museum of Art & History @ The McPherson Center, Santa Cruz, CA.

Santa Cruz Mountains winemakers at the BATF hearing to establish the Santa Cruz Mountains AVA.
L to R: Front row - Val Ahlgren, Linda McHenry, Dexter Ahlgren, Doug Fletcher, Eleanor Ray
Back row - Dave Benion, Nat Sherrill, Paul Draper, Russ Walker, Ken Burnap, Jan Sherrill, Chuck Devlin

After obtaining land and planting his vineyard on the mountain, Ray was faced with another problem: he wouldn't have grapes for winemaking for at least five years. Casting about for another source, he took over the maintenance and grapes of Rixford's La Questa Vineyard in 1946. At the same time, he took cuttings from La Questa to his vineyard on the mountain. For the next thirty years, he spent his time creating Cabernet Sauvignon, Chardonnay and Pinot noir vintages in the French tradition. The best of those wines have a reputation for quality to this day. At the same time, he continued to harangue the winemakers from his mountaintop pulpit, frequently rousing their anger, but getting his point across nonetheless. By all accounts, a visit to his home was both fascinating and unpredictable. On at least one occasion he sent someone packing back down the mountain in the middle of dinner.

In 1960 Ray incorporated the vineyard and winery and sold shares to the new corporation, Mount Eden Vineyards. The premise was to raise money and to found a domain in the French manner with several vineyards under the corporate umbrella. He would tell everyone how things were to be done and the shareholders would just relax and enjoy the ride. Amazingly enough, this arrangement worked for seven years, although Ray objected to having his privacy infringed upon by these other "owners" and made them unwelcome at the winery. Eventually, the other owners had enough of the situation and made a bid to take over the corporation. In 1972, after years of court battles and meetings, Martin Ray lost everything except for a small piece of property and his home. Ill and disheartened, Ray died in 1976.

At the same time that Ray was building his mountaintop winery, the first of several waves of winemakers began to arrive in the Santa Cruz Mountains, many adding winemaking to their full time jobs in other professions. Dermatologist David Bruce purchased land on Bear Creek Road and began his search for the perfect Pinot noir in 1964. Hewlett-Packard engineer Dan Wheeler started his bonded winery in 1955 using grapes from a vineyard planted on part of the old Jarvis estate. In 1959 another set of engineers from Stanford Research Institute purchased the land and winery that was to become Ridge Vineyards in 1962. Bob Mullen and Bob Groetzinger began to make wine from remnants of the historic La Questa vineyards in Woodside in 1961.

Many of the wineries that were established in the decade of the 1970s are still in operation and are covered in this book, including: Ahlgren, Cronin, McHenry, Santa Cruz Mountain Winery, Page Mill Winery, Obester, P M Staiger, and Silver Mountain. Some of the wineries no longer exist or have moved to other locations, but their contribution to the continuation and success of the area wineries should not be overlooked.

In 1972 Bob Roudon and Jim Smith bonded the Roudon-Smith Vineyards winery near to where Dr. John Stewart had his winery in the 1890s. Although they remained small, they worked with other newcomers to the area and participated fully in promoting the Santa Cruz Mountains wineries and their communities. The Roudon-Smith winery was put up for sale in 2003, although the tasting room is being maintained by Glenwood Oaks. Jan and Nat Sherrill opened Sherrill Cellars in 1973 and were instrumental in the creation of the Santa Cruz Mountains American Viticultural Area (AVA), although they are no longer in the winery business. It's rumored that they are now raising llamas in Southern California.

The Locatelli/Eagle Rock winery was re-opened in 1976 under its new name, the Sunrise Winery, by Keith Hohlfeldt and Eugene Lokey. Lokey left the operation in 1976 and was replaced by Ron and Rolayne Stortz. When the historic winery burned down, the Stortzes left the location and moved to the Picchetti Ranch in 1983; Jim Beauregard took over their lease on the property. Peter Pourroy's establishment was also resurrected in 1976. Dan and Robin Gehrs, with support from Victor Erickson, ran Congress Springs Vineyards until the late 1980s when it was sold to a corporation. After a period of inactivity, the vineyard became Savannah-Chanelle.

Other wineries came and went during this time frame, including Cloudstone in Los Altos Hills, Cook-Ellis in Corralitos, Devlin in Aptos (Devlin has since become a winemaker in Idaho.), Crescini and Nicasio in Soquel, Frick in Santa Cruz, Grover Gulch in Santa Clara County and Walker in Palo Alto. The comedian, Dick Smothers, made a brief appearance in the area, operating the Vine Hill Winery from 1977 to 1979.

In the early 1970s, a small group of Santa Cruz Mountain winery owners (Bob Mullen from Woodside, Ken Burnap from Santa Cruz Mountain Vineyards, Dexter Ahlgren from Ahlgren Vineyand and Dave Bennion from Ridge) began to have dinner together to exchange ideas, problems, and collectively order winemaking supplies. The Sherrills joined in 1973 and the Santa Cruz Mountain Vintners Association was born. Over the next seven years the group, particularly Bennion and Burnap, covered the mountains to determine the boundaries they wanted to propose to the Bureau of Alcohol, Tobacco and Firearms (BATF) for the Santa Cruz Mountains AVA, one of the earliest AVAs to be determined by altitude. Although there was much discussion with owners around the mountains, there were some that disagreed with the boundaries, particularly the altitude boundary of 400 feet on the western side of the mountains. Nonetheless, the group went forward with these boundaries and the BATF approved the proposal. During the hearing process, Kathryn Kennedy lobbied to have her parcel included in the appellation, and it was.

There were, however, several significant wineries that were left out of the appellation, including Bargetto, Felton-Empire (Hallcrest), Devlin, and Aptos Vineyards. The Santa Cruz Mountain Vintners Association decided that only those wineries actually in the appellation could be part of the association. Looking back with twenty-five year hindsight, Bob Mullen says this was probably not the best choice, but it was the one that was made. As a consequence, Devlin and several others formed the Santa Cruz County Winegrowers Association to include those not in the appellation. Finally, during his term as president of the Santa Cruz Mountain Vintners Association, Mullen urged the integration of the two associations and the Santa Cruz Mountains Winegrowers Association was born.

By the end of the 1970s, there were about 30 wineries in and around the mountains. Several more became bonded in the 1980s and are still in existence today. Later in that decade, Jim Beauregard successfully lobbied for an AVA within the Santa Cruz Mountains: Ben Lomond Mountain. McHenry is the only winery physically in the Ben Lomond AVA, although Bonny Doon retains a tasting room and Beauregard is creating wine based on grapes from within the AVA.

Throughout the 1990s and early 2000s, wineries continue to appear and join the association. By mid-2003, there were 54 wineries total – a number that astounds people like Ken Burnap and Bob Mullen when they hear it. Most of these wineries will remain small, primarily by design. Some will fade as people grow older and find no successor for their romantic, but laborious lifestyle. But the camaraderie and fine wine that can be found in the Santa Cruz Mountains will always welcome those who want to create their niche in this world.

Photo courtesy Charles L. Sullivan

(Endnotes)
[1] Holland, Michael R., <u>Late Harvest, Wine History of the Santa Cruz Mountains, The Late Harvest Project, p.56.</u>

The Wineries

Wineries in the Santa Cruz Mountains range from under 500 cases of production a year to over 250,000 cases. Both corporations and individuals own wineries. Some are open every day; some are never open. Some are reasonably easy to get to and some take a commitment to trust that the dirt road carved into the side of a mountain actually leads to a winery. Whatever the situation, traveling to a Santa Cruz Mountain winery is an interesting proposition.

The wineries that follow are divided into three groups: the east side of the mountains, west side and mid-mountain. Keep in mind that roads through the mountains wind through narrow valleys, sometimes diminishing to a path between two elderly redwoods. (A designated driver is definitely recommended.) You should plan on three, possibly four, wineries in a trip, depending on when you go and which wineries you choose. To gain access to the most wineries, plan to travel during the Santa Cruz Mountains Winegrowers Association events described in the final chapter of this book.

As you plan your trip, consider incorporating some other activities:

- Mid-peninsula Regional Parks for hiking
- Filoli Estate for garden tours
- Mountain Home Winery or San Gregorio General Store for music
- Half Moon Bay, Santa Cruz and other cities for golfing
- Saratoga and Soquel for antique shopping
- Santa Cruz for the Boardwalk and wharf
- Felton for the Roaring Camp Railroad
- State beaches along Highway 1
- Big Basin and Henry Cowell State Parks for first-growth redwoods
- Shakespeare Santa Cruz

Can't find the wine or winemaker of your choice? Check out winemakers' dinners in area restaurants such as Shadowbrook in Santa Cruz. Call or email your favorite winery to find out their schedule or get on their mailing list for future events. You can attend some very special events by developing relationships with small winemakers and joining their wine clubs.

At the end of the day, there are many stores and restaurants that carry a good selection of Santa Cruz Mountains wines.

Happy and safe traveling!

Sempervirens Falls, Big Basin Sate Park

For more information

California State Parks
www.parks.ca.gov
800.777-0369

Mid-peninsula Open Space District
www.openspace.org/

Half Moon Bay Coastside Chamber of
Commerce and Visitor's Bureau
www.halfmoonbaychamber.org
650-726-8390

San Gregorio General Store
www.sangregoriostore.com
650-726-0565

Filoli Estate
www.filoli.org
650-364-8300

San Jose Convention and Visitor's Bureau
www.sanjose.org
888-SAN-JOSE

Saratoga
www.saratoga-ca.com

Mountain Home Winery
www.mountainwinery.com
408-741-2822

Aptos Chamber of Commerce
www.aptoschamber.com
831-688-1467

Santa Cruz County
www.scccvc.org
800-833-3494

Santa Cruz Parks and Recreation
ww.santacruzparkandrec.com

Shakespeare Santa Cruz
www.shakespearesantacruz.org
831-459-2159

Aptos Chamber of Commerce
www.aptoschamber.com
831-688-1467

Santa Clara Convention and Visitor's Bureau
www.santaclara.org
800-272-6822

San Jose Convention and Visitor's Bureau
www.sanjose.org
888-SAN-JOSE

Saratoga
www.saratoga-ca.com

Mountain Home Winery
www.mountainwinery.com
408-741-2822

Restaurants with good selections of Santa Cruz Mountains wines; starred restaurants have a better-than-average selection.

East Side

Woodside
Buck's
John Bentley's*

Menlo Park
Flea Street Cafe

Palo Alto
St. Michael's Alley*
Cafe Pro Bono

Portola Valley
Parkside Grille

San Jose
A.P. Stump's

Campbell
Buca Restaurant*

Saratoga
The Basin
Bella Saratoga
Big Basin Bistro
Plumed Horse
Sent Sovi
Viaggio

Los Gatos
Cafe Marcella*
California Cafe
Los Gatos Brewing Company

West Side

Pescadero
Duarte's Tavern

Davenport
New Davenport Cash Store

Boulder Creek
Boulder Creek Country Club
Scopazzi's*

Ben Lomond
Ciao Bella

Felton
Mama Mia's
Trout Farm Inn

Scotts Valley
Cafe Max (Hilton)

Santa Cruz
Black's Beach Cafe
Cafe' Lola
Casablanca
Chocolat
Cloud's Downtown
Gabriella Cafe
Hollins House
Ideal Bar and Grill
O'mei
Oswald's
Pearl Alley Bistro
Ristorante Avanti
Riva's

Soquel
Michael's on Main*
Theo's

Capitola
Ostrich Grill
Shadowbrook

Aptos
Cafe Rio
Southern Exposure Bistro

Stores with good selections of Santa Cruz Mountains wines

Woodside
Robert's Market

Saratoga
Gene's Quito Market
Uncorked

Los Gatos
Whole Foods

Santa Cruz
Pleasure Point Wine Shop
Shoppers Corner

Capitola
41st Avenue Liquors

Aptos
Breadstix Deli and Wine
Deluxe Foods

21

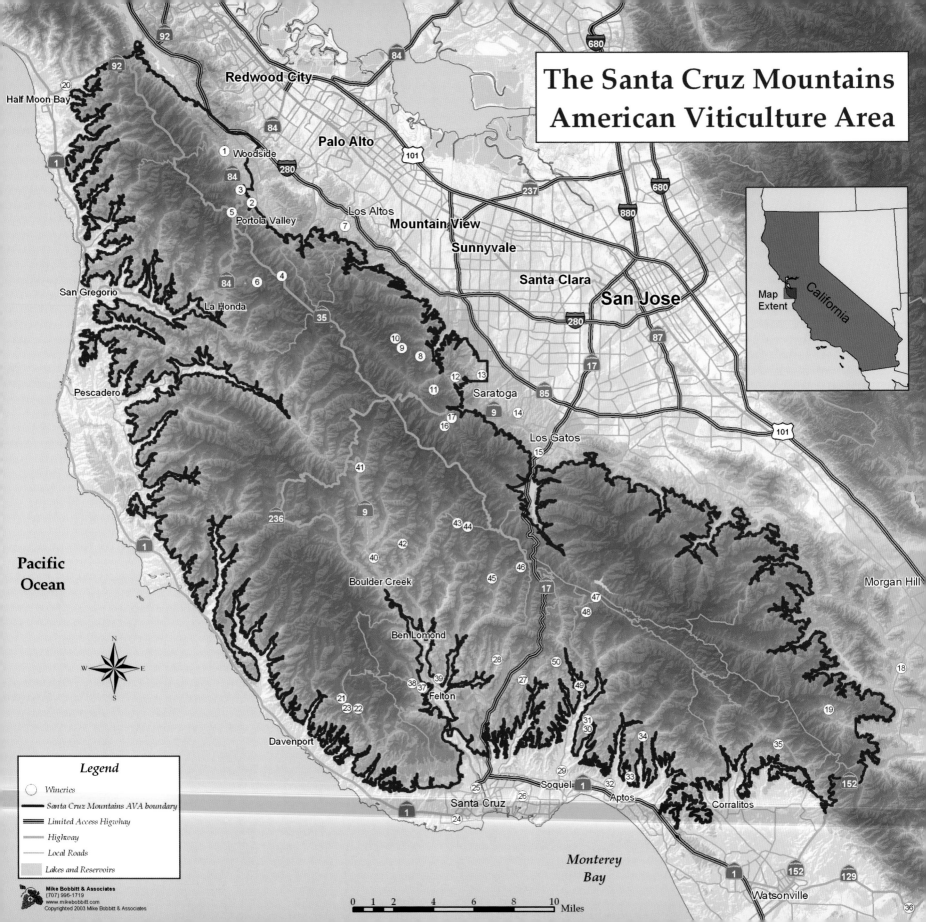

East Side

1. Woodside Vineyards
2. Cronin Vineyards
3. Chain D'Or Vineyards
4. Thomas Fogarty Winery and Vineyards
5. Michael Martella Wines
6. Clos de la Tech
7. Page Mill Winery
8. Picchetti Winery
9. Fellom Ranch Vineyards
10. Ridge Vineyards
11. Mt. Eden Vineyards
12. Cooper-Garrod Vineyards
13. Kathryn Kennedy Winery
14. Lonen and Jocelyn Wines
15. Troquato Vineyards
16. Savannah-Channel Vineyards
17. Cinnabar Vineyard and Winery
18. Clos LaChance Wines
19. Fernwood Cellars
20. Obester Winery

West Side

21. Bonny Doon Vineyard
22. Beauregard Vineyards
23. McHenry Vineyard
24. Pelican Ranch Winery
25. Storrs Winery
26. Thunder Mountain Winery
27. Clos Tita Winery
28. Glenwood Oaks Winery
29. Bargetto Winery
30. Hunter Hill Vineyards and Winery
31. Soquel Vineyards
32. Aptos Vineyard
33. Salamandre Wine Cellars
34. Trout Gulch Vineyards
35. Windy Oaks Estate Vineyards and Winery
36. River Run Vintners

Mid-Mountain

37. Hallcrest Vineyards/ Organic Wine Works
38. Cordon Creek
39. Anderson Vineyard
40. Equinox
41. Ahlgren Vineyard
42. P•M Staiger
43. Byington Vineyards and Winery
44. David Bruce Winery
45. Zayante Vineyard
46. Generosa
47. Burrell School Vineyards
48. Silver Mountain Vineyards
49. Osocalis
50. Santa Cruz Mountain Vineyards

The Wineries

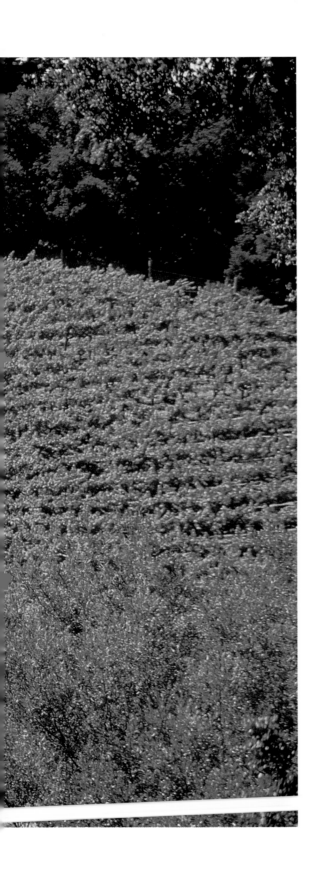

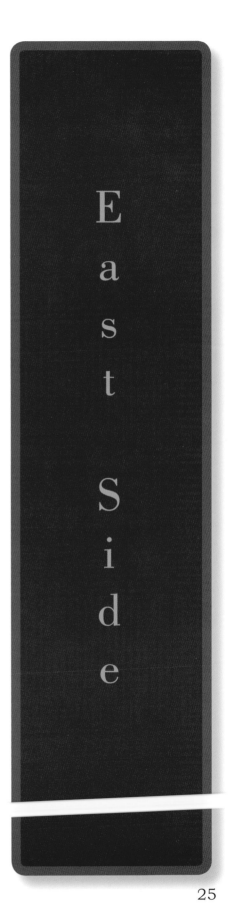

East Side

Woodside Vineyards

Woodside Vineyards

340 Kings Mountain Rd.
Woodside, CA 94062
Phone: (650) 851-3144
Fax: (650) 851-9556
email: info@
 woodsidevineyards.com
Web site:
www.woodsidevineyards.com
Annual Production: 2000 cases
Winemaker: Brian Caselden
Winery Owners: Bob Mullen and
Brian Caselden

Access
Open by appointment only

Tastings
No tasting fee
Wines: Chardonnay, Cabernet
Sauvignon, Pinot noir, Zinfandel,
port, champagne

Sales of wine-related items? No

Picnics and Programs
Small weddings up to 60 people;
Participates in Santa Cruz
Mountains Winegrowers
Association events

For Bob Mullen, one of the elder Santa Cruz Mountains winemakers, the future looks bright. "I don't see another large winery starting in the mountains," he says, "mostly mom and pop operations, which is the way it should be."

Mullen provides a link between some of the oldest viticultural history in the mountains and the present. In 1884, E.H. Rixford planted a vineyard he called La Questa in Woodside that lasted well into the 20th century when it was revived by Martin Ray (see the history chapter for more information on Ray) in the 1940s. After that, housing development took over and parts of the vineyard wound up in suburban backyards.

In 1957 a friend of Mullen's, Bob Groetzinger, discovered some of Rixford's vines, cleaned them up, and made wine with them. Mullen joined the venture and purchased his Woodside property in 1961 -- the best investment he's ever made. By 1963 their home winemaking quantity was pressing the legal limits, so Woodside Vineyards was bonded and Mullen joined the ranks of winemakers with other full time jobs.

Bob Mullen and Brian Caselden

From the beginning, Woodside Vineyards concentrated on small vineyard management (from around half acre to about three acres), maintaining as many parts of the old La Questa vineyard as they could find, as well as others in Woodside. They currently manage about 24 vineyards, and consider these vineyards their "estate." According to Mullen, he can taste the Woodside earth in their wines, a flavor that is different from other parts of the Santa Cruz Mountains.

Woodside Vineyards only produces estate wines, concentrating on Cabernet Sauvignon, Pinot noir, Zinfandel and Chardonnay, with some production of sparkling wine and port. Brian Caselden, winemaker and part owner, follows Mullen's approach to hand-tailored wines. "We have complete control from the vineyard to the bottle," he says. Every wine requires a different regime of winemaking, but in general the reds are unfined and unfiltered, while the whites are sterile filtered and fined. Caselden is using 60 % French oak barrels with the rest American oak and an average of 30 % new barrels each year.

Bob and Brian are exploring the idea of a second tier of wines (the label to be graced by Mikey, the winery dog) developed from wines that don't contain the quality they want for their premium wines.

Mullen was active in the Santa Cruz Mountain Vintners Association from its formation, serving as president of the association when it merged with the Santa Cruz County Winegrowers Association. "They were two groups with the same interests at heart," he says. He was also on the Board of Directors of the Wine Institute for ten years, working with them to increase the number of states that allow wine shipments from California. He recently joined in that group's celebration of the repeal of Prohibition in 2003.

In spite of his energy, Mullen recognizes that he is getting older. In 2001 he created a Limited Liability Corporation (LLC) to sell shares in Woodside Vineyard.

That way, he can relax and enjoy his favorite part of the winemaking process -- drinking the wine he makes.

Cronin Vineyards

Duane Cronin's love affair with wine began when he was five years old. While his parents weren't wine-lovers, they would buy a bottle whenever they entertained. Children in the Cronin household were expected to eat and drink what was placed on the table during these occasions. Duane discovered at an early age that he preferred wine over milk and couldn't wait for company to come to visit again.

Throughout his entire engineering career, Cronin never lost interest in wine. While working in Washington, D.C., he discovered French wines. A move to California introduced him to California wines. Finally, a job shift to northern California in the mid-1970s made him realize, "By golly, I could grow grapes here!"

Spring bud break at Cronin

Duane planted his tiny vineyard in Woodside, but realized he didn't want to wait five years to make wine. So he began to look for grapes, obtaining Zinfandel in 1976 from Charlie Wagner of Napa's Caymus Winery. By 1980, Cronin was making more than the 200 gallons allowed to him as a home winemaker. Unwilling to give up his hobby, he bonded C—

In addition to his tiny vineyard, Cronin still purchases grapes to make his wine. This gives him room to explore the differences that various vineyards impart to the fruit. While tasting his four Chardonnays, for example, you become aware of the subtle differences between the wines produced from the Sonoma, Monterey and Santa Cruz Mountains AVAs. Although he strives to keep his own vineyard organic and work with others that have organically grown fruit, Cronin is another vineyard owner who feels the cost and paperwork of organic certification is too high.

There's a different style of winemaking for each wine that he makes, according to Cronin. He wants to enhance the flavor of the fruit with as little intervention as possible. The Chardonnays are barrel fermented *sur lees* in French oak for eight months, and stirred occasionally. Cronin insures malolactic fermentation to add complexity to their structure and avoid sterile filtration. While Cronin doesn't fine or filter his reds, he tries to avoid a "snow scene in the Chardonnay." To do this he fines using a mild bentonite solution, providing just enough to clear the wine without destroying the flavor. The Chardonnays are also put through a coarse filtration (.8 microns).

Duane Cronin treats his reds to a very traditional winemaking process, fermenting in an open-topped fermenting tank with hand punch down. The wine is then put in a combination of French and American oak for storage in Cronin's cool, damp cellar.

Cronin strives to make a wine that goes well with food. To him this means that there is enough acid to cleanse his palate completely, yet enough complexity to make the wine interesting and memorable. If you are drinking his wine with a friend over a good meal, the highest compliment would be for you to lean to your dinner companion and say, "What do you taste in this wine?" and have the answer be something unpredictable.

Cronin Vineyards

11 Old La Honda Rd.
Woodside, CA 94062
Phone: (650) 851-1452
Fax: (650) 851-5696
Annual Production: 2000 cases
Winemaker: Duane Cronin
Winery Owner: Duane Cronin

Access
Open by appointment only
Please write above address to get on mailing list

Tastings
No tasting fee
Wines: Chardonnay, Cabernet Sauvignon, Merlot, Pinot noir

Sales of wine-related items? No

Chaine D'Or Vineyards

Chaine D'Or Vineyards

Woodside, CA
Phone: (650) 851-8977
Annual Production: 500 cases
Winemaker: Anne Anderson
Winery Owners: Jerry and Anne Anderson

Access
Open by appointment only

Tastings
No tasting fee
Tours available by appointment only
Wines: Chardonnay, Bordeaux blend

Sales of wine-related items? No

Picnics and Programs
Participates in Santa Cruz Mountains Winegrowers Association events

When Anne Anderson emigrated from Britain, she brought a great love of vineyards and wine. So, when her husband, Jerry, needed something that would help reduce stress and provide more exercise, she suggested planting grapes. In 1987 they put in two acres of vines: Chardonnay and Cabernet Sauvignon with small amounts of Merlot, Cabernet Franc and Petite Verdot for blending.

Since Jerry had a farming and ranching background from his youth in Texas, he was put in charge of the vineyard. "I'm better at driving tractors and pruning," he says. As he goes about his tasks with the help of the vineyard dog, Jesse, Jerry enjoys a view of the vineyard which also provides great beauty. On a sunny day, the San Francisco Bay is spread out below and the fog folds into the mountains surrounding the vineyard.

There was also the matter of the tools required to make wine. "We need the same equipment as a large winery," Anne says, "just smaller." She also notes that the winery looks glamorous, but requires a lot of cleaning, and the only way to clean the press is to get inside it.

The Andersons make the decision to pick grapes based on sugar, but sugar content is determined by tasting as well as looking at brix. According to Anne, the sugar of a ripe grape tells you that there's no kind of waiting allowed -- you need to pick it right at that moment.

The couple decided to name their winery after the historic name for the east side of the Santa Cruz Mountains, *Chaine D'Or* (golden chain). Following some negotiations with a French winery also called, *Chaine D'Or*," the winery was bonded in 1990. Their fee for the use of the name? They have to send two cases of the wine to France every vintage.

Jesse in the Chaine D'Or Vineyard

Anne is charge of the winery. "She has a good palate," Jerry says, although according to Anne, learning to make wine wasn't always a smooth progression. Jerry had the scientific background; they took some courses at UC Davis and acquired some books on viticulture and winemaking. As always in the mountains, they received help from local vineyard owners.

Anne and Jerry Anderson enjoy the Santa Cruz Mountains winemakers. "There's a fraternity that doesn't exist in many other industries," Anne says. They have a passion for the process of making wine, knowing if one year isn't great, they get another chance the following year. The wine they sell to their neighbors and small stores around Woodside, reflect the love and attention Jerry and Anne pay to their grapes and the winemaking process.

Thomas Fogarty
Winery and Vineyards

19501 Skyline Blvd.
Woodside, CA 95062
Phone: (650) 851-6777
Fax: (650) 851-5840
email: info@fogartywinery.com
Web site:
www.fogartywinery.com
Annual Production: 15,000 cases
Winemaker: Michael Martella
Winery Owner: Dr. Thomas
Fogarty

Access
Open Thursday to Sunday 11-5

Tastings
$5.00 tasting fee, includes logo
glass
Wines: Chardonnay,
Gewurztraminer, Cabernet
Sauvignon, Merlot, Pinot noir,
Sangiovese

Sales of wine-related items? Yes

Fogarty Futures Club
Two bottles four times a year
of limited production wines;
complimentary tastings; annual
event; 15% discount on bottles;
20% discount on cases

Picnics and Programs
Event site for weddings, corporate
events, winemaker dinners and
other events;
Participates in Santa Cruz
Mountains Winegrowers
Association events

Thomas Fogarty Winery and Vineyards

Elegance greets you at the Thomas Fogarty Winery from the moment you enter the gate. The drive to the parking lot brings you past a lily encrusted pond dominated by two white swans. As you walk past well-tended vines from the lot to the tasting room, San Francisco Bay spreads out before you like a blanket for a giant's picnic. The tasting room itself is a comfortable room with blond wood walls, brick red tiled floors and a stunning view.

One of Thomas Fogarty Winery's swans

Over thirty years ago, when Dr. Thomas Fogarty purchased the 325 acres that became home to the winery, only the view of the bay and a small cabin existed on the property. Fogarty taught heart surgery at Stanford Medical Center when he was introduced to the pleasures of wine-making. A self-proclaimed tinkerer, he invented the Fogarty embolectomy catheter which he patented in 1969. This instrument is a type of balloon catheter that provided less-invasive relief to heart patients than previously had been available.

Fogarty planted the first grapes in 1978, focusing on the Burgundian grapes of Pinot noir and Chardonnay. The completed vineyard covers 25 acres and also includes small lots of Merlot and Sangiovese. In 1980, Fogarty bonded the winery and hired Michael Martella to be the viticulturist and winemaker. Martella has been there ever since. As he says with a smile when he points to the great views from his place of work, "Look around you."

As is typical for a mountain site, there isn't a great depth of topsoil. Most of the foot of soil is composed of loam and sand without too much clay, giving the vines good drainage before they need to fight through the bedrock of sandstone and shale. The vines are primarily grafted to AxR #1 rootstock, using Wente clones for the Pinot noir and UC Davis #5 for the Chardonnay.

Martella's aim in the vineyard is to use sustainable farming whenever possible. He uses drip irrigation in some parts of the vineyard, dry-farming others. He pays close attention to the vines, keeping track of how they look, particularly as harvest time approaches. The decision to pick is based on scientific evidence of sugar and acid content as well as a dollop of an experienced taste of a ripe grape. The process of getting the grapes to ripeness can be a harrowing one since Santa Cruz Mountains' fruit changes from year to year based upon climatic conditions. The colder climate provides the fruit structure that Martella needs for his wines, but he has developed a trellising system that captures the sunlight to insure that the grapes are ripe before the winter rains arrive. Even then, he finds himself keeping a close eye on the sky as he picks. While the primary grapes for Fogarty wines come from the estate vineyard, Martella also contracts with local growers for Cabernet Sauvignon, Cabernet Franc and Merlot.

Martella's goal is "to make delicious wine." This is the driving force behind his viticultural and winemaking methods and is most important to his decision making process. Fogarty wines express the cold climate; they are more structured with higher acid than is usually found in wine and demonstrate flavor based more on the soil than the fruit. This is a different style from many of the fruit-forward wines that people think of when they think of California wines.

When you walk through the door of the Fogarty winery on your way to the tasting room, you are on a walkway suspended over one of the two barrel rooms. Take a moment to look down over the polished steel fermentation tanks and neatly stacked barrels. The barrels are 100% French oak for the Pinot noir, a combination of French and American oak for the Chardonnay and Santa Cruz Mountains Merlot, and 100% American oak for the Cabernet Sauvignon.

Martella's approach to winemaking changes from year to year based on the characteristics of the fruit. For example, he'll choose the amount of new oak he'll use for fermentation based on those qualities. He admits, though, that lately he's been backing off on new oak, reaching for a softer balance in his wines. He uses commercial yeast to start fermentation and makes decisions of filtration and fining on an individual basis. A recent Pinot noir was neither filtered nor fined.

Martella and Tom Robinson, the cellar master, find their jobs fascinating. "It's intellectual and physical work," Robinson says. There is a beauty and challenge in watching the dynamic changes in the vineyard and tasting the results of their labor in the bottle of wine.

Fogarty wines are designed to be a "drinking wine." Martella wants consumers to be "really satisfied and happy that they chose a Fogarty wine when they are at the bottom of the bottle." Martella isn't the type of winemaker to be satisfied with his existing creation, however, and he looks forward to better and better wines. He believes that there is a direct relationship between the focus he places on the wine and its quality. Dr. Fogarty is also dedicated to the finest wine possible, willing to invest when needed and is, in Martella's words, "great to work with."

In addition to the winery, the site provides excellent facilities for corporate events and weddings. The buildings hang on the edge of the mountain, with dramatic views of the vineyard, the bay and the valley.

The vineyard is surrounded by many fine hiking trails, some of which can provide 360 degree views of the San Francisco Bay and the Pacific Ocean. Stopping at the Fogarty Winery is the perfect way to end a beautiful day in the Santa Cruz Mountains.

Thomas Fogarty vineyard

Michael Martella Wines

Michael Martella Wines

17287 Skyline Blvd.
Box 103
Woodside, CA 94062
Phone: (650) 851-6777
Web site:
www.michaelmartella.com
Production: 1500 cases
Winemaker: Michael Martella
Winery Owner: Michael Martella

Access
No winery access

Tastings
Wines: Syrah, Zinfandel

Picnics and Programs
Participates in Santa Cruz
Mountains Winegrowers
Association events

Michael Martella is the long time winemaker at Thomas Fogarty Winery. With that distinction comes a certain style and consistency of wine. In the French tradition, Michael has also developed his own label to be able to express his talent in a different way. Although not always a common practice in the US, it is a tradition that is seeping its way into the winemaking communities.

While Fogarty wines are generally estate varietal wines, Michael's wines are driven towards blends of the same varietal that will give him the expression of the grape he's looking for: "a rich, lush body and a lingering finish." He's looking for a very "up-front wine" with his own label.

The beauty of a winemaker that tries different styles of wine is that it benefits the consumer. Tasting a Fogarty wine and a Martella wine side by side is an expression of personality.

Michael Martella

Clos de la Tech

T.J. Rodgers likes to make things. "There are two things that make humans happy," he says, "thinking and doing." As founder and CEO of Cypress Semiconductors, a Silicon Valley chip company, he does plenty of thinking. What does he do? He makes Pinot noir.

Born in Oshkosh, Wisconsin, Rodgers attended Dartmouth College in New Hampshire, followed by a move to Stanford in 1970. He claims that wine in Oshkosh in the 1960s only came with a screw top. The first California red wine he tasted was in the town of Gilroy. This experience inspired trips to Napa, where he visited small wineries. In 1972 a clerk at Beltramo's Liquors in Atherton introduced him to red Burgundy wine and "the hook was set."

"The French wines have more dimension, more layers that we [Californians] are just developing," claims Rodgers.

Fast forward twenty-four years. Rodgers has founded Cypress Semiconductors, become an opinionated spokesperson of Silicon Valley and amassed enough money to invest in "The Great American Pinot Noir." Understanding detail is imperative in chip development and likewise, Rodgers delves into every detail possible in wine development as he begins the process.

At his home in Woodside, T.J. Rodgers put in over 2,000 vines at what became the Domaine du Docteur Rodgers vineyard of Clos de la Tech winery. The soil is "five feet of clay on top of serpentine bedrock on a hilltop, 400 feet above sea level." He needed a rootstocks that were resistant to all manner of ills, as well as being able to tolerate wet lands in winter and dry clay in summer. The rootstocks he chose include Riparia Gloire, Millardet et de Grasset 101-14 and Courderc 420A. The clones were Dijon 113 and 115.

Rodgers' careful attention to the minutest detail carries over to vine spacing which is exactly 66 inches between rows and 40 inches between vines. He keeps the height of the vines low and the yield extremely low.

Since 1994, Rodgers has put in two more vineyards: Domaine Valeta named after his

Domaine Lois Louise

domestic partner and Domaine Lois Louise named after his mother. Plants in these vineyards are jammed into a 42 inch by 36 inch space.

Rodgers' most recent vineyard was built on steep slopes (up to 60 percent grade) in the Santa Cruz Mountains. To maintain the vineyard process he wants, he's built special machinery in conjunction with German firms to carry vineyard workers up and down the steep rows for pruning, maintenance and harvest. Three 300-foot caves are also being built on the property for the new winery, bunkhouse and living quarters.

As might be imagined, the engineering expertise of T.J. Rodgers comes into play in his winemaking. He understands and explains his winemaking decisions precisely, including chemical diagrams to show the origin and effect of Brettanomyces and other winery nasties. His creativity is demonstrated by his experimentation with the production of a near-Burgundian wine rich with oily, round tannins, dark color and berry and perfume scents. His signature is a silicon chip embedded in wax on the neck label of special reserve Clos de la Tech wine.

T.J. Rodgers is committed to his vision of Pinot noir and won't spare any effort to obtain the results he wants. "I can afford to be patient," he says. The wine will go to up-scale restaurants and to those willing to pay a premium price. Not everyone will be in on the allocation.

In the meantime, T.J. Rodgers will keep making his great American Pinot noir.

Clos de la Tech

Woodside, CA
email: tjr@cypress.com
Annual Production: 100 cases
Winemaker: T.J. Rodgers
Winery Owner: T.J. Rodgers

Access
No tasting room available
Wine: Pinot noir

Page Mill Winery

Page Mill Winery

13686 Page Mill Rd.
Los Altos Hills, CA 94022
Phone: (650) 948-0958
email:
Dane@pagemillwinery.com
Web site:
www.pagemillwinery.com
Annual Production: 3000 cases
Winemaker: Dane Stark
Winery Owners: Stark family

Access
Open by appointment only

Tastings
Wines: Chardonnay, Sauvignon blanc, Cabernet Sauvignon, Merlot, Pinot noir, port

Sales of wine-related items? No

Picnics and Programs
Evening tastings; classes
Participates in Santa Cruz
Mountains Winegrowers
Association events

Dane Stark wants people to know that winemaking is his "real job." In an area filled with Silicon Valley executives, backyard grapes and hobby vintners, he's proud of that fact, as well as the fact that Page Mill Winery is family owned and run.

Dane's parents, Richard and Ome Stark, began Page Mill Winery in 1976 when Richard quit his job at a technical firm in the valley. They'd been introduced to wine for the first time in the early 1970s because Richard's brother-in-law, surprised that they knew nothing about it, decided to educate them. A few years later, Richard was jacking up the house with his son, Eric, and building a cellar for a winery underneath.

Dane Stark

Over the next five years, Richard learned where to source his grapes, built his skills as a winemaker and gradually increased production. From the very beginning, the Starks promoted food and wine pairings, either at restaurants, or, more commonly, at dinners in the wine cellar. They found this was a good way to explore the flavors that went together with Page Mill wines.

During this time winemaking was primarily a family venture with all of the children, Eric, Tor, Inger and Dane, involved in some aspect of creating wine. As they grew up, the children moved away from the family venture, except for Dane.

Only eight years old when he began working as winery helper, Dane wasn't really interested in the business until he spent his junior year abroad at the University of Bordeaux. There he fell in love with wine, enjoying the French *joie de vivre*, the romantic view of the pleasures of the table, and the perception of wine as food. He appreciated the less commercial aspects of winemaking -- the winery owner's attachment to the earth.

When he returned to California in 1991, Dane began to work with his father and take courses at the UC Davis extension school. It was a gradual adjustment to the winery life -- both father and son were trying to determine if it would be a lasting endeavor. But Dane discovered that he liked all the aspects of making wine: "the work of the vineyard, the creative production of wine and even dressing up nice and being the center of attention." He's embraced his father's ideas of food and wine pairing, continuing the dinners and adding educational events about wine tasting. Dane delights in enticing people to enjoy all the pleasures of the table, including wine.

Although Page Mill has a few wines made from grapes in the Santa Cruz Mountains, the Starks have had long relationships with vineyards in Santa Barbara and Alexander Valley. Making wines from the same vineyards, according to Dane, helps you learn about the difference weather conditions can make from vintage to vintage.

Dane is focused on high quality wine, yet acknowledges that the vintner merely stewards the wine from the vineyard to the bottle, putting finishing touches on God's creation without stylistically changing the wine.

And that, he says, is a full-time job.

Picchetti Winery

Picchetti Winery

13100 Montebello Rd.
Cupertino, CA 95014
Phone: (408) 741-1310
email: info@picchetti.com
Web site:
www.picchetti.com/
Annual Production: 9000 cases
Winemaker: Jeff Ritchey
Winery Owner: Leslie Pantling

Access
Daily 11-5

Tastings
$5 tasting fee, good towards wine purchase;
Tours available by appointment only
Wines: Chardonnay, Cabernet Sauvignon, Merlot, Pinot noir, Zinfandel, sparkling wine

Sales of wine-related items? Yes

Picchetti Wine Club
Four bottles three times a year from $45- $65 each shipment.
(free shipping)
Special events

Picnics and Programs
Picnic area; access to Mid-peninsula Open Space Preserve;
Live music on Sundays;
Event site for small weddings, parties, winemaker dinners and other events;
Participates in Santa Cruz Mountains Winegrowers Association events

Leslie Pantling was originally looking for a place to store a barrel of homemade wine, when she decided instead to buy a winery complete with century-old Zinfandel vines and peacocks.

In 1872 Vincenso Picchetti emigrated from Italy and began to work for Santa Clara College tending their vines. Within ten years, his brother, Secundo, joined him. The brothers purchased 160 acres on the lower part of Monte Bello Ridge in 1877 for $1500. The land included acres that are now under water in the Stevens Creek Reservoir and a nearby quarry. The winery planning started in 1892 and it was completed in 1896. Its upper floor, used during the Picchetti era for dehydrating fruit, was also used for social events, including Hector Picchetti's (Vincenso's grandson) wedding. This room is now the tasting room for the new Picchetti Winery.

Vincenso eventually purchased Secundo's share of the winery and left it to two of his sons, John and Antone. The two men and their families lived in the "big house" on the property. The winery shut down during Prohibition except for wine made for home consumption. With two families, that was 400 gallons a year. After repeal, the Picchettis were quick to start up their operation again, primarily selling wine by filling their customers' jugs. The Picchettis were an integral part of the community, since many people made a weekly trip to the winery well into the 1950s. The Bennions (one of the founders of Ridge) remember getting wine there and Louise Cooper of Cooper-Garrod Winery remembers Picchetti wine at her wedding in 1941.

Leslie Pantling pouring at "Wine with Heart" event

John and Antone's shares passed to their sons, Hector and Elio during the 1950s. The cousins tried to keep the winery going, but there wasn't enough income to maintain it. In 1963 they closed the winery down, although Hector and Elio maintained ownership of the property, continuing to sell wine up until 1972. They sold their unused wine grapes to Ridge and other fruit to Sunsweet. In 1976, with a slump in grape and fruit prices, the cousins decided to sell the property and winery. The Mid-peninsula Open Space Preserve bought the remaining Picchetti property and buildings in December 1976, with a provision to lease nine acres (six acres covering the buildings and three acres of Zinfandel vines) in 25 year intervals. The first people to take advantage of that lease were Rolayne and Ronald Stortz.

The Stortzes had previously been part of a partnership running Sunrise Winery on the Locatelli property by Eagle Rock in the Bonny Doon area of the Santa Cruz Mountains. After a series of proposals and bids, they were able to lease the property in 1983. From that point on, there was a lot of work rebuilding and preserving the old buildings. In 1984 the Stortzes began to make Zinfandel from the grapes on the property. They built their business until the mid 1990s.

Leslie Pantling lives up Montebello Road, just below the Ridge winery. A single mom with three kids, she ran an international sales force for Sun Microsystems. She also had grapevines on her land, and was selling the grapes to Ridge. In the mid-1990s she decided to try her hand at home winemaking (although she admits she's a poor winemaker), and needed a place to store her first barrel. After hearing the proposal from the Stortzes to buy the winery, she gave it serious thought. While she liked the idea of owning her own business, she knew the situation was complicated by the need to take care of historic buildings and the public who came to enjoy them, as well as the nearby trails. In 1998 she made her decision and took over the winery, giving Sun Microsystems a year's notice of her departure.

Decision made, she plunged into work, purchasing equipment and hiring a staff of "great people" to get her started. She also put her marketing skills to work, selling tastings of five local wines for $5 to build a base of customers while she created her first wines.

Michael Dashe, previously with the Ridge Lytton Springs operation, helped her get started and in September 1999, she began to sell her first wines. The original wines were made at custom crush facilities while she revamped the winery. Her first production at the Picchetti facility began in 2000.

Because Leslie had worked with Ridge on vineyard maintenance, she knew the quality of farming she wanted from her own grape suppliers. Her own vineyard fruit, of course, now goes into Picchetti wine rather than Ridge wine. It took her a while to develop relationships with other Santa Cruz Mountains growers, but she is now in a position where 70% of her fruit comes from Monte Bello Ridge.

Picchetti Tasting Room

Her wine is single vineyard designated, with concentrations on the 120-year-old Picchetti Zinfandel, as well as the Cabernet Sauvignon and Chardonnay from her vineyard. She gets other grape varieties based on her ability to obtain the quality of fruit she wants. An interesting sidelight is a sparkling wine imported from Italy.

She recently hired Jeff Ritchey, former winemaker at Clos LaChance. Jeff believes in hands-off winemaking, interfering with the process as little as possible.

A trip to Picchetti is a trip back in time. In addition to the warm ~~~~ ~~~~ ~~~~~~ ~~~~~~~ ~~~~~~~, there are a few distinctive treasures at the location. The first is a legacy from John Picchetti, a bird lover and collector.

Peacocks strut their stuff around the property, occasionally taking an artful pose on picnic tables or fence posts. They've been known to take a stroll up Montebello Road, so it pays to be careful when you drive.

The other noteworthy piece is a carved cask in the tasting room. Although its origins can't be documented, the Picchettis believed that it was a prize that Pierre Klein received at the St. Louis Fair in 1904. Klein was a well-known vintner in the late 1800s who owned property further up Montebello Road.

As one of the closest wineries to Silicon Valley (an easy drive off Interstate 280), the warm and friendly atmosphere makes it easy to plan return visits. There are trails to hike, and space to throw a Frisbee or play a game of bocce. Plan a picnic complete with a freshly purchased bottle of wine from Picchetti Winery.

Zinfandel Trail - Picchetti Ranch Open Space Preserve

Fellom Ranch
Vineyards

17075 Montebello Rd.
Cupertino, CA 95014
Phone/Fax: (408) 741-0307
Web site: www.fellom.com
Annual Production: 1000-1500
cases
Winemaker: Roy Fellom III
Winery Owner: Roy Fellom III

Access
Open by appointment only

Tastings
No tasting fee
Wines: Cabernet Sauvignon,
Zinfandel, port

Sales of wine-related items? No

Picnics and Programs
Participates in Santa Cruz
Mountains Winegrowers
Association events

Fellom Ranch Vineyards

"You have to be put together a certain way," Bud Fellom says, "to work in this business. It's incredibly demanding, nothing but work." Bud is constantly battling the environment and forces of nature. Deer, coyotes and raccoons continually work at getting past the perimeter fence. Gophers launch subterranean attacks. Every so often Bud finds himself trying to herd deer from the vineyard. "And deer don't herd very well," he says. "They go every way but the way you want them to go."

Even though there are sacrifices, Bud loves the agricultural lifestyle. "I'm tuned into the seasons. The vineyards are my annual clock." Bud can tell the exact time of year by where the sun hits the vines and their stage of development. To him, growing vines is like a marriage; you need to pay attention or they will wither.

of the final product. The soil that underlies his vineyard contains limestone, serpentine and Franciscan chert. The earth is clay and sandy loam; the former is poor for the grapes. Believing that new technology helps the vintner achieve his goals in the bottle, Bud works in soil additions to improve the nourishment of the vines. While not an organic viticulturist, Bud doesn't add anything to the soil that is going to impact the environment, but only looks at micronutrients to fortify soil content.

A former pre-med student at UC Berkeley, Bud's knowledge comes from an education in biological science as well as a full program in enology and viticulture through UC Davis Extension. His winemaking philosophy is that you need to have a clear understanding of organic chemistry in order to gather a chemical profile of the wine, as well as a sensory appreciation of its taste, smell and color. He begins his wine blending with the grapes in the vineyard and adjusts the blend during fermentation, paying particular attention to

Paula and the Jazz at Fellom Ranch open house

The first Roy S. Fellom, a two-time California State Senator, purchased the property on Monte Bello Ridge in 1929 and passed it on to his son, Roy Fellom, Jr. In the early 1980s Roy Jr. and his son, Bud, replanted the existing vineyard with Cabernet Sauvignon, Merlot and Petite Verdot. Today Bud and his wife, Karen, manage all aspects of the Fellom Ranch Vineyards operation.

Like many vintners, Bud believes that what happens in the vineyard is an important element

the amount of acid in the wine, including ratio of total acid to pH. Since his wine selection consists entirely of reds, tannin management is also important.

Bud believes that the Santa Cruz Mountains are a unique place to make wine, and within that special place, Monte Bello Ridge stands out. The vineyards and winery are an integral part of Bud Fellom's world. The amount of wine he produces allows him to experience the life style that he wants for himself, his wife and three children.

Ridge Vineyards

If you can survive the trip up Montebello Road, a twisting, turning, narrow slice of road carved into the side of a mountain, you will come to one of the Santa Cruz Mountains' most renowned wineries: Ridge Vineyards. In addition to the winery, spectacular views of Silicon Valley, the San Francisco Bay and, on a clear day, San Francisco itself await you. The tasting room and surrounding picnic area provide room to reflect on the historical roots of the location -- old vines and the original Ridge winery.

Paul Draper, Ridge's winemaker, stresses the tremendous differences between the mountain climate and any other winemaking region in California. The climate is cooler than Napa, and the soil is markedly different from the Santa Clara Valley and Livermore. Draper quotes geologic studies to the effect that Monte Bello Ridge was formed 60 or 70 million years ago near the equator; it sheared off the Pacific Plate as it slid under the North American plate and remained on the mountains. The result is a subsoil of fractured limestone overlain with ferrous sedimentary rock -- perfect for providing a mineral undertone to the wine.

In 1959, four scientists from Stanford Research Institute International (SRI) purchased eighty acres, 25 of which were 10-year-old Cabernet Sauvignon vines and a dilapidated old winery building on a dirt road close to the top of Monte Bello Ridge. (This property, frequently called the lower winery, is the location of the tasting room today.) The men and their families immediately went to work building fences and cultivating the vines that were there. Their first vintages were sold to a local winemaker, Mario Gemello, but one of the owners, Dave Bennion, also took some of the grapes and began to make wine. In 1962 the partners re-bonded the winery and the bumpy road to fame began.

Throughout the next decade, the partners expanded the business, becoming a corporation and purchasing the "upper winery." Osea Perrone, a San Francisco physician, had planted vines and built a home and winery on the property in the late 1800s.[1] The Ridge owners purchased this historical building and replanted the surrounding vineyards that had been abandoned during Prohibition. In 1969 Paul Draper joined the firm and moved production to the upper winery in 1971.

The reputation of the wines and winery grew from that point. By the mid-1980s, with two partners in their early seventies, the founders decided that the time had come to step back. Several parties were interested in buying the winery, including three large multi-national corporations who hoped to make Ridge their flagship wine. In late 1986 one of the members of the Otsuka family from Japan met with the founding partners and Draper. The Americans found Otsuka's views on winemaking and goals for Ridge were in harmony with theirs and Ridge

Paul Draper

was sold by the end of the year. Unfortunately, Dave Bennion was killed in a traffic accident on the Golden Gate Bridge a mere two years after retirement.

In 1970, Paul Draper became Ridge's head winemaker; he maintains this position today as well as that of Chief Executive Officer. Although his university degree was in philosophy, Draper became intrigued by the wine business, reading everything he could on viticulture and wine production. He and a partner, Fritz Maytag, set up a winery in Chile in the 1960s, but left after several years due to changes in the country's economic climate, subsequently joining Ridge. Through the 1970s, Draper imprinted his own style and philosophy on the winery.

Draper calls himself a practical winemaker. He approaches each part of the process -- choosing a vineyard to participate in Ridge wines, selecting the lots for the single vineyard designation and blended vineyard wines, deciding fermentation method and selecting barrels -- with a methodology aimed at retaining the underlying structure and complexity of the wine. Ridge wines are made with aging in mind.

Like many Santa Cruz Mountains winemakers, Draper is a man with definite opinions on how his grapes and wines should be handled. He separates blocks of grapes throughout the fermentation process until the final blending process, when only a portion are chosen for blending into Ridge's top wines.

Always a tinkerer (he calls himself a frustrated architect), Draper has been designing the equipment used in the winery operations from the beginning. He believes that smaller fermentation tanks create more intense flavors. They are also easier to lift up and empty directly into the press -- Draper believes that this method of handling is far easier on the skins and seeds than any type of pumping. The pumps used for the aging wines are smaller versions of those used in the food industry to pump tomatoes without breaking the skins.

Once the natural primary and secondary fermentations are finished, the wines are put into air-dried American oak barrels, built by both French and American coopers. Never complacent, Draper keeps some of the wine aside to test new coopers and woods, insuring that he maintains the quality he wants.

Throughout the aging process, Draper and his tasting team analyze the wines to determine the blend of each vineyard's grapes "that best highlights the vineyard's distinctive character and quality." Ridge's top wines are vineyard designated. In the Santa Cruz Mountains, the second tier wines are all from the estate and small neighboring vineyards on the ridge. Their top Zinfandel wines, principally from their vineyards in S...

designates; the second tier moves to blends of softer wines from a number of vineyards.

To determine the assemblage of the wine, Draper's small team does blind tastings and votes on parcel lots to include. Everyone is encouraged to express themselves and hold to their opinions. If Draper's opinion is different from everyone else's, which is rare, he doesn't force that opinion. Rather the group assembles another day and tries again. "I don't want us to develop a house palate," he says.

Although Draper is the driving force behind the winery and wines, he knows he doesn't do it alone. He points to the dedication of everyone who participates in the operation, from the pruner in the vineyard to the person washing out the tanks to his fellow team members who head production and viticulture. These people are the "only reason we make good wine," he says.

Draper is passionate about his occupation and winemaking in general. He loves the synergy that happens when the blends are built by the winemaking team, one lot at a time. He likes to talk and write about what he's doing at Ridge -- admitting that sometimes he does get on a soapbox. But primarily he feels part of a natural process, not trying to build a commodity, but "rather guiding a transformation from the fresh fruit to a complex and delicious wine." The cycles of the year dictate what he does and the fruit from the land dictates what he produces. He plans to continue on with Ridge, attempting to make "some of the finest wine in the world."

(Footnotes)

[1] See History for more information

Ridge Cabernet Sauvignon

Mount Eden Vineyards

As one of the oldest continuously operated wineries in the Santa Cruz Mountains, Mount Eden is steeped in the history of the Santa Cruz Mountains. Winemakers who began their winemaking careers in the 1950s or 1960s invariably mention the time they met, learned from or were dismissed by Martin Ray, the original owner of Mount Eden. Many credit Ray with influencing their winemaking style. Ray's difficult disposition, however, caused him to lose his kingdom on the hill to his partners in 1972.[1]

Between 1972 and 1982, the winery was run by Dick Graff (in addition to his responsibilities at Chalone Winery in Monterey). Since 1981, however, the Mount Eden vineyard and winery has operated under the leadership of Jeffrey Patterson.

Jeffrey Patterson

Patterson went to school at UC Berkeley, majoring in biology in the early 1970s. Between 1975 and 1980, having discovered wine and become passionate about it, Jeffrey decided to go into wine production. For the next two years he took a crash course at UC Davis, and in 1981 got his first job at Mount Eden.

Forty acres of vineyard

on Chaine D'Or ridges before sliding down the thirty to forty degree slopes. The steep slopes pose a challenge to the vine grower, requiring concerted efforts against erosion and paying the high cost of maintaining such efforts. This mountaintop vineyard is the essence of Mount Eden wine. The soil (if you can call it that) is Franciscan brown shale with very little topsoil. Because the vine has to work hard to hold on in these conditions, it's smaller than normal. The water also drains well, producing small berries, naturally stressed.

High mountaintop weather is fickle and Patterson must pay attention to the logistics of the vineyard. A heat wave can change his plans suddenly. Yet these stressful conditions create the taste that Patterson, and many others, seek. This old vineyard must be maintained, however, and Patterson is replanting where needed, providing younger rootstock and more density between the vines.

Because of the small size of the winery, grapes can be dumped by gravity into the crusher and press that are located part way down the mountain. The liquid is pumped into the tank, but after that there is no more pumping. Patterson believes in a non-interventionist approach to the winemaking process. Mount Eden's barrels (50% new each year) reside in caves bored out in 1991. "Caves are really good for wine," says Patterson. The temperature and humidity are right for their development.

Fining is reserved for non-estate Chardonnay. All Chardonnays are filtered for clarity. "Mount Eden Chardonnays age for a long time," Patterson says.

Jeffrey believes that a bottle of Mount Eden wine should evoke a sense of place - - a viticultural island suspended over the mountains. Mount Eden's history, as well, is captured in the essence of every bottle.

Mount Eden vineyards, both before and after Martin Ray, have produced long aging wines with interesting character. These are vineyard wines, demonstrating the vineyard's character rather than a blend. Indeed, the Chardonnay and Pinot noir are the longest lineage estate wines in California. It is this essence of history that Patterson preserves in every bottle of Mount Eden wine.

[1] See History for more information

Mount Eden Vineyards

22020 Mt. Eden Rd.
Saratoga, CA 95070
Phone: (888) 865-9463
Fax: (408) 867-4329
email: info@mounteden.com
Web site:
www.mounteden.com
Annual Production: 18,000 cases
Winemaker: Jeffrey Patterson
Winery Owners: Mount Eden partnership

Access
Open by appointment only

Tastings
No tasting fee
Wines: Chardonnay, Cabernet Sauvignon, Pinot noir

Sales of wine-related items? No

Picnics and Programs
Participates in Santa Cruz Mountains Winegrowers Association events

Cooper-Garrod Vineyards

22645 Garrod Road
Saratoga, CA 95070
Phone: (408) 867-7116
Fax: (408) 741-1169
email: wine@cgv.com
Web site: www.cgv.com
Annual Production: 3,000 cases
Winemakers: George Cooper; Bill Cooper
Winery Owners: Cooper-Garrod family

Access
Open weekdays 12-5;
 weekends: 11-5

Tastings
No tasting fee
Wines: Chardonnay, Viognier, Cabernet Franc, Cabernet Sauvignon, Claret (Cabernet Sauvignon and Cabernet Franc blend),

Sales of wine-related items? Yes

Cathedral Club
Two bottles four to six times a year from $30 to $75 each shipment;
Additional discounts available.

Picnics and Programs
Picnic area;
Next to Garrod Farms Riding Stable;
Participates in Santa Cruz Mountains Winegrowers Association and Santa Clara Valley Winegrowers Association events

Cooper-Garrod Vineyards

If you enjoy hiking or horseback riding, combining these activities with a visit to the Cooper-Garrod winery is an easy matter. The Garrod Farms Riding Stable offers trail rides over 120 acres of vineyards and chaparral on their own property as well as along 23 miles of riding trails on the Fremont Older Mid-Peninsula Open Space Preserve. Hiking is also available in the Open Space Preserve that surrounds the Cooper-Garrod stables and winery.

R.V. Garrod purchased 65 acres in Saratoga in 1893, and he and his descendants added acreage over the next 50 years until it amounted to 240 acres of fruit trees and hay fields. Louise Garrod, granddaughter of the original settlers, married George Cooper, a research test pilot who was to become Chief of Flight Safety Operations with NASA in 1941. The first vineyards of Cabernet Sauvignon were planted 31 years later by George and the rest of the Cooper-Garrod clan shortly before his retirement in 1973.

Currently, the family owns 120 acres, having sold the other 120 acres to the Mid-Peninsula Open Space Preserve in the early 1980s. Twenty-eight of the remaining acres are now vines.

Located within 20 minutes of Martin Ray's property, it was natural for George to look to Martin for information on vineyard management and wine-making. "I was friendly with him," George says. They traded wine stories and flying stories and George always wiggled his wings when flying over the Mount Eden winery. Ray supplied George's Vineyard (the name of the original two acres) with Cabernet Sauvignon from plants he had developed from cuttings from Paul Masson's vineyard.

Three additional acres of Cabernet Sauvignon were planted on a 35-degree hillside above the winery in 1989; six more acres were planted on a similar slope in 1991. Prior to this, the family branched out to Chardonnay vines grafted onto St. George rootstock: four acres in 1979 and one acre in 1980. This was followed by five acres of Cabernet Franc in 1985. Once again, George was able to obtain historic cuttings, this time from the original Pourroy vineyards (now Savannah-Chanelle). Syrah, Viognier and Merlot make up the remaining seven acres.

The estate, including the winery, has always been a family affair. Jan Garrod, George and Louise's nephew, manages the stables and vineyards. The vineyards are dry-farmed, although they do give the vineyards "a shot of water after the grapes are harvested in the fall." The family has embraced sustainable farming, with Bill Cooper, George's son, participating in a two-year study to develop the Wine Institute's Code of Sustainable Winegrowing Workbook. Bill is also the assistant winemaker. His wife, Doris, is the marketing director and his sister, Barbara, supervises the tasting room and finances.

Cooper-Garrod "Fruit House"

In addition to working with Martin Ray, George also developed his trade by working with winemakers in Napa, as well as Bordeaux and Burgundy, France. He also took extension courses at UC Davis. When asked for his winemaking strategy, however, George is likely to quip, "What's so difficult? You crush grapes, put them into a container and let them ferment."

In reality, it has taken the Garrod-Cooper family a great many years to reach the point where they were willing to put their finest efforts forward to the public. While they began making wine in 1975, they didn't release the first vintage until 1994. The first step in their commercial operation was to lease equipment and part of a cave at Mount Eden Vineyards from 1991 to 1998. In 1998 they constructed a barrel room and moved all the winemaking onto their property.

"There are so many aspects to making wine," George says. "You can see the wine develop through the whole process. There's satisfaction seeing people enjoy the product."

The Cooper-Garrod Vineyards and Garrod Farms Riding Stables are on a small ridge in the Saratoga hills. A trip to the facility allows you to enjoy the sounds of horses clip-clopping as their owners take them to or from the stables, as well as a soft view of the Santa Clara Valley below.

The tasting room is in a building that is designated the Fruit House -- built over 75 years ago to store dried prunes and apricots prior to shipment. It was also used as a social hall for dances and gatherings after the fruit shipped. Over the years, the eucalyptus used for the foundation and the roof have been replaced, but the rest of the structure remains the same.

Within the walls, there are fascinating exhibits of old-time Saratoga, as well as pictures from George's flying days. Recipe boxes near the tasting bar contain Doris Cooper's tried and true recipes -- free for the taking. In addition to the traditional winery equipment, books and accoutrements, there are unique items for sale -- paintings and craft items from various relatives.

If you are hiking or riding, the large jug of water is inviting, as are the snacks that are frequently available. There isn't any pretense at this wine bar -- the wine is a part of the life that surrounds you -- part of open space, agriculture and history.

Although the property is the longest single-family owned property in the mountains, the winery is a relative newcomer in terms of longevity; their first commercial vintage was 1994. The family's entry and continued growth in the wine business is slow and deliberate; they are careful of financial investment and conscientious about preserving the heritage for future generations. George is enthusiastic about Bill's growth as a winemaker, as are other winemakers in the appellation. Bob Mullen, for example, felt comfortable leaving his position on the Wine Institute board of directors only after he could pass on the seat to one of the "young fellows" in the area -- Bill Cooper.

A trip to Cooper-Garrod offers a great sense of extended family on the property, reaching back over a hundred years. George and the rest of the family all invite you to share the fruits of their labor.

Cooper-Garrod tasting room

Kathryn Kennedy Winery

13180 Pierce Way
Saratoga, CA 95070
Phone: (408) 867-4170
email: cabernet@
   kathrynkennedywinery.com
Web site:
www.kathrynkennedywinery.com
Annual Production: 5000 cases
Winemaker: Marty Mathis
Winery Owner: Kathryn Kennedy

Access
No tasting room available
Wines: Cabernet Sauvignon,
Syrah, Lateral (red blend)

Wine Clubs
"Sting of Pearls": one, two or
three bottles of special bottlings
by Kathryn Kennedy from $60 to
$150 a shipment

Picnics and Programs
Participates in Santa Cruz
Mountains Winegrowers
Association events

Kathryn Kennedy Winery

On clear winter days you can find Marty Mathis pruning his seven acre vineyard in Saratoga, totally oblivious to the large suburban homes surrounding him. Mathis is very dedicated to his pruning, convinced that "cane pruning, although the slowest and most costly method, gives fruit of the most desirable nature: smaller berries, better color and more concentrated wine."

Marty Mathis began making the wine in 1981. From the beginning he had definite ideas about how wine was made, sometimes in conflict with Kathryn. The secret, he believes, is to produce wine that's "going to go in the right direction." While he pays attention to brix, he is also concerned with how much acid there is in the wine, claiming that it influences the way a wine tastes.

The Kathryn Kennedy estate label remains the flagship wine, hand managed from the vineyards to the small winery on the property. Marty picks by blocks within the vineyard and the grapes

Marty Mathis

Marty was trained this way by his mother, Kathryn Kennedy. Kathryn planted the vineyard in 1973 with 3,333 Cabernet Sauvignon cuttings she obtained from David Bruce for a nickel each. She enlisted her extended family and planted each of them on their roots. Her main reason for creating a vineyard was to keep the land from being subdivided for housing; the way to do that was to keep the land agricultural. It was either Christmas trees or grape vines and since she didn't want to be so busy at Christmas time that would take time away from her young family, grape vines became her choice.

It wasn't until 1979 that Kathryn Kennedy made her first wine. Right from the beginning she decided it was going to be a premium product. And, right from the beginning she decided to put her name on the winery. "It was my effort, my gamble, my land, my money. If David Bruce and Martin Ray could do it, so could I." Because of the small lots, Kathryn Kennedy wine is considered a "cult wine" in the Santa Cruz Mountains.

are dumped directly into the crusher and de-stemmer. He avoids the use of a must pump to prevent manhandling the fruit. The grapes in the small, open topped fermenters are hand punched down. Marty uses a variety of times and methods during fermentation, from short skin contact to extended maceration. This gives him the ability to blend within his estate grapes, providing optimum richness to the wine.

Two other tiers within the winery are the Lateral St. Emilion Bordeaux style blend and small lot wines. The small lot Cabernet Sauvignons are made from grapes planted in backyards in the Santa Cruz Mountains.

Passionate about his wine, Marty loves his job. "There's a complexity to it. I can spend a lifetime learning. I like to doodle around on the farm." He admits that a winemaker needs to tolerate uncertainty; that he isn't really in control. Marty works hard, however, to guide the wine into the result that he wants. Consequently, he maintains that there is a "large amount of love per bottle."

Lonen and Jocelyn Wines

Tucked deeply into a residential area in Saratoga, Susan's Vineyard is not obvious to the casual observer. It is, in fact, one of the many "backyard vineyards" that have been scattered throughout the Saratoga hills since the 1880s. In this case the vineyard is behind the home of Susan and Lonen Curtis.

The Curtises have spent much of their life in Silicon Valley's tech industry, all the while harboring a strong feeling for the earth and its fruits, and a belief in sharing that bounty with good friends. As they moved closer towards retirement, they realized that they could have the life they wanted -- creating something with their hands that results in a real product. For role models, they have the elegant wines of neighboring Kathryn Kennedy and Ridge wineries. Clos LaChance had propagated the idea of small vineyards in Saratoga. So with high hopes, they began.

The Curtises cleared the land in their back yard and obtained three or four gunny sacks of 1600 dormant Cabernet Sauvignon bench grafts. Soil analysis showed them that they had sandy loam, clay and rock, with enough resistance to provide stress, but also an area that drained well. Optimistic, they arranged a planting party, planted vines and began their farming life. After four or five weekends, however, Lonen realized what most new vineyard owners realize -- it's a lot of work -- and they hired a vineyard manager.

Owning a vineyard has brought them a form of satisfaction that their previous work had not. "The vineyard is addictive," notes Susan. Although she isn't able to participate in the daily running of the family business, she does enjoy going out in the early morning fog to the valley of her vineyard; experiencing a sense of isolation in the heart of the neighborhood. Both of the Curtises find it awe inspiring to walk in the vineyard and realize they are in the middle of future wine.

The vines were planted in 2000; their first estate wines are expected to be available in 2004. In the meantime, Lonen and their daughter, Brandi Jocelyn (Curtis) Pack have boned up on their winemaking skills, taking advantage of distance learning from UC Davis. They have also taken the step of purchasing superior quality fruit and creating wine with consultant winemakers who use a custom crush arrangement in Napa. Their goal is a consistent quality wine that resonates a sense of place. "We're not going to sell a bad wine," Lonen says.

Susan and Lonen believe that pairing wine with food takes both elements to a new level. Lonen admits that food without wine is no longer complete. Their sense of elegance is reflected in the wine, and also in everything that surrounds it, including the bottle. However, the Curtises hold that there is no room in the wine industry for wine snobs. Their philosophy is that the best wine is the wine you like, period.

They have found great satisfaction in the wine country lifestyle. We like "sharing the joy we derive from our vineyard and wine with friends we've met through the process," Lonen says. Their only regret? They wish they'd done it sooner.

Lonen and Susan Curtis with daughter Brandi

Lonen and Jocelyn Wines

15127 Sperry Lane
Saratoga, CA 95070
Phone: (866) LJWINES
Fax: (408) 395-9942
email: lon@jocelynwines.com
or brandi@jocelynwines.com
Web site:
www.jocelynwines.com
Annual Production: 3000 - 4000 cases
Winemaker: Joshua Krupp
Winery Owners: Lonen and Susan Curtis

Access
Open by appointment only

Tastings
No tasting fee
Wines: Chardonnay, Cabernet Sauvignon, Zinfandel port, Meritage blend

Sales of wine-related items?
Through web site only

Jocelyn Cellars Wine Club
Contact Jocelyn Cellars for more information

Picnics and Programs
Participates in Santa Cruz Mountains Winegrowers Association events

Troquato Vineyards

Troquato Vineyards

Los Gatos, CA 95033
Phone: (408) 866-6700
Annual Production: 500 cases
Winemakers: Angelo and George
Troquato
Winery Owners: Angelo and
George Troquato

Access
No tasting room available
Wines: Chardonnay, Cabernet
Sauvignon

Picnics and Programs
Participates in Santa Cruz
Mountains Winegrowers
Association events

Angelo Troquato was a little kid in an Italian neighborhood in Scranton, Pennsylvania in the late 1930s. A wine-drinking family, the only downside to the experience was that his family knew they couldn't make wine from Pennsylvania grapes. "We knew the best grapes came from California," he says.

To get around that problem, he and his uncle would go down to the Lackawanna Railroad station when the boxcars of grapes came in from the West. He remembers the large flavored Zinfandel and the Muscat grapes. The first crush of grapes would be for the family. For a second press, they'd add sugar and water to the must and crush again. This was the wine they would sell. If the grapes allowed it, the process would be repeated as many times as possible.

The lease ran out in 1993 and Angelo leased another piece of property in Campbell. Unfortunately, that land is now under Highway 85. Since 1995, Angelo has been making wine with other people's grapes. He looks for vineyard owners whose grapes form the foundation of wines that are considered the best.

His son George helps him with the winemaking. George is the winemaker at Cinnabar and is also a wine consultant at Testarossa Vineyards in Los Gatos. Working in the vineyard since he was twelve, George was undeterred and he went to the California Polytechnic Institute and received a degree in agronomy.

The Troquatos do as little filtering and fining as possible and barrel age in American oak. "We like American oak," Angelo says. "It's very, very good and not too expensive." Their goal is to make a wine that is memorable.

Angelo Troquato pouring at Vintner's Festival '03

After college, Angelo came West to find land for his own vineyard and garden.

He leased seven acres in Saratoga to use for his vineyard. For the next 30 years he grew and sold grapes to the vintners in the area. However, in 1984, he couldn't find buyers for his fruit. At that point he also decided that wine in the bottle had a longer life span than grapes on the vine. His decision to start a winery coincided with his retirement from his "day job." Troquato Vineyards was bonded in 1985.

Troquato Vineyards isn't making the volume of wine they once were due to the slump in the market. But having lived through various ups and downs of the winery market all his life, Angelo knows the winery can continue as a small family owned winery. "It's a nice business, nice people," he says. "It's a more relaxed, civilized way of living."

Savannah-Chanelle Vineyards

23600 Congress Springs Rd.
Saratoga, CA 95070
Phone: (408) 741-2934
Fax: (408) 867-4824
email: tastingroom@
   savannahchanelle.com
Web site:
www.Savannahchanelle.com
Annual Production: 12,000 cases
Winery Owners: Michael and
Kellie Ballard

Access
Open daily 11-5

Tastings
$5 tasting fee;
$12 fee per person for tours
Wines: Chardonnay, Cabernet
Franc, Pinot noir, Zinfandel

Sales of wine-related items? Yes

Insiders Club
Two or four bottles four times a
year at about $40 or $75 each
shipment;
Special events

Picnics and Programs
Walk through redwoods, fish in
stream and picnic on hillside;
$5 Friday afternoon tours and
tasting
Weddings and corporate events
available;
Participates in Santa Cruz
Mountains Winegrowers
Association events

Savannah-Chanelle Vineyards

Michael and Kellie Ballard were interested in developing a business in which the whole family could participate when they came back to the San Jose area from Washington, D.C. Their dream involved an agricultural environment, but they realized that Silicon Valley held few opportunities for this type of endeavor. Then they discovered that the old Congress Springs Winery in the Santa Cruz Mountains was for sale.

The romantic magic of owning a winery instantly appealed to the Ballards. They had a love of wine and enjoyed studying about it and collecting it. The winery for sale included 58 acres in the hills above Saratoga with a great home site and a century-old historic property. "There was a basket of factors – overwhelming and compelling," Ballard says.

Pierre Pourroy planted the first vineyards in this location in 1892 with the help of his brother, Eloi. Pierre was a well-respected winemaker in his time. The Pourroy family expanded the vineyards through the years, adding a gravity-flow winery in 1917. The Zinfandel vines planted in 1910 and the Cabernet Franc vines (the oldest in the world outside of the Loire Valley and Bordeaux) which were planted in 1920 are still vibrant today.

After surviving Prohibition, the Pourroys made red table wine and sold the grapes to surrounding wineries. They stopped making wine in the 1940s, but continued to sell their grapes to such wineries as the Novitiate. In 1976 Daniel and Robin Gehrs created a partnership with San Jose businessman, Victor Erickson and purchased the winery and renamed it Congress Springs. Their winery was operated sporadically until the Ballards bought it in 1996.

The Ballards wanted a new identity for the winery but didn't want to settle for a mundane name, so they combined the names of their daughters to create Savannah-Chanelle. The Ballards feel this name is a great icon for the family business and lifestyle they wish to achieve.

As an interesting side note, the Ballards changed the name of their winery in 2000 from Savannah-Chanel to Savannah-Chanelle to settle a lawsuit with Chanel, Inc., the fashion and cosmetics corporation.

The Ballards have a great respect for the history they have inherited, as well as a sense of responsibility for future generations. While they are not deliberately organic in their vineyard practices, they are careful with what they do. Very few chemicals are used, just enough to provide a healthy environment for the plants.

Savannah-Chanelle tasting room

In addition to the historic vineyards, the Ballards are "obsessed with Pinot noir." They have planted Pinot noir vines along steep slopes on their own land, but also search out other appellations with outstanding Pinot noir grapes, such as the Santa Lucia Highlands and the Sonoma Coast. Over 85% of Savannah-Chanelle wines are Pinot noir, both single vineyard designates and regional blends. Ballard's mission is to showcase the range of California *terroir* with this single varietal wine. The other wines are based on the historic varietal grapes of Cabernet Franc and Zinfandel, or other outstanding grapes that have become available to the winery during a particular vintage, including grapes from a new Syrah vineyard high in the Gavilan Mountains. Ballard has also planted Paul Masson's Corton Charlemagne Chardonnay clone on the property.

Many people are involved in the process of winemaking -- all the way from the vineyard to the tasting room -- at the Savannah-Chanelle Winery. This ensemble effort, Ballard claims, allows the winemaker's palate to be augmented with exposure from others, avoiding a "house palate." He often brings in consulting winemakers to add spice to the winemaking process. Sometimes it's a "rock star" consultant, sometimes a European winemaker. He'll bring in consultants just for a day, to taste and comment and listen to the team. Ballard believes the process leads to "self-evident and compelling wines."

Wine Display

A journey to Savannah-Chanelle is a step into history. The tasting room was built in 1912 in the middle of the surrounding vines. Redwoods tower over the parking lot, adding to the feeling of age. Along with the wine, the Ballards try to display the integral lifestyle around which wine is wound. "Wine is the womb for all the great and wonderful things in the world," Ballard says. For art, food, and music, wine is the companion. To that end, you will often find a pianist at the winery during the weekends, playing jazz or classical melodies on the grand piano. A nice touch is a collection of children's books and a drawing table in a corner of the spacious tasting room. Few winery owners admit their customers have progeny.

A Mediterranean-style chateau with a view over Silicon Valley is also available for weddings, picnics, barbecues and corporate events. Food and wine pairings are another focal point at Savannah-Chanelle.

The Ballards will continue to develop their property and facilities with an aim toward increasing the quality of their wines. Michael is focused on allowing his customers to have a viscerally distinctive experience. The wines, he believes, are "high on the yummy factor." His daughters, seven and twelve, are a little young to take on the work of the winery, but should they make that decision, they'll have a head start on many of their neighbors.

A mere 3.3 miles from the heart of Silicon Valley, a trip to Savannah-Chanelle brings you to the peace and serenity of a good wine region. In addition to spending time in a historic winery, close to century-old vines, you can walk redwood forests of their own. Sun shines gently on the hillside. If you aren't careful, you can slip back in time, forgetting the hectic life of the early twenty-first century. Michael Ballard would have it that way.

Cinnabar Vineyards and Winery

23000 Congress Springs Rd.
Saratoga, CA 95071
Phone: (408) 741-5858
Fax: (408) 741-5860
Email: suzanne_frontz@
  cinnabarwine.com
Web site:
www.cinnabarwine.com
Annual Production: about 15,000 cases
Winemaker: George Troquato
Winery Owner: Tom Mudd

Access
Open by appointment only

Tastings
No tasting fee
Wines: Chardonnay, Cabernet Sauvignon, Merlot, Pinot noir, Mercury Rising (a Cabernet Sauvignon/Cabernet Franc blend)

Sales of wine-related items? Yes

Picnics and Programs
Participates in Santa Cruz Mountains Winegrowers Association events

Cinnabar Vineyards and Winery

Driving to the top of Cinnabar's perch requires patience and caution. The road twists and turns up the mountain through vineyards to the state-of-the art winery. As you get out of your car, take a moment to look at the panoramic view of Silicon Valley from the top of Tom Mudd's 30-acre Chardonnay, Pinot noir and Cabernet Sauvignon vineyard, originally planted in 1984.

As you might guess from the gleam of stainless steel tanks and meticulous arrangement of the winery (built in 1987), Tom was an engineer. In fact, he is a former Senior Research Engineer from SRI (Stanford Research Institute International) whose consuming interest in his hobby led him from a one-acre vineyard in Woodside to his present site.

The estate vineyard produces about 3,000 cases of wine a year, with another 12,000 cases coming from fruit grown in a Central Coast appellation. Mudd planted 22 acres of the estate in 1984 on AxR#1 rootstock. For bud wood he used Mount Eden cuttings, since he was a fan of the wine coming from Martin Ray's vineyard. However, the combination was not good for the Cinnabar vineyard. The rootstock was susceptible to phylloxera and the cuttings only produced about 1.5 tons of grapes an acre. As a result, Mudd is in the midst of replanting with new rootstocks and new clones. "The magnesium in the vineyard is excessive," Mudd says. The new rootstocks favor the uptake of potassium which will prevent an overabundance of magnesium in the grapes. Mudd is also planting less Chardonnay and increasing the amount of Cabernet Sauvignon vines.

The Cinnabar vineyard manager, Ron Mosely, notes while the 60 to 90 inches of annual rainfall may have provided rich soil for Silicon Valley agriculture, it left only a foot of topsoil at the mountaintops. In the world of grapes, however, this is good news for the quality of the wine, since it results in small, flavorful berries that go into the creation of Cinnabar's exquisite Chardonnay, Pinot noir and Cabernet Sauvignon.

Tom Mudd enjoys the challenges of the winegrowing business; and there's always a challenge, always something new to learn. A better understanding of grapes and wine science is emerging, helping vineyard managers understand the optimum time to pick and prune, as well as harvest. This new knowledge provides an "ever changing palate from which we paint our pictures," Tom says. He's also passionate about sustainable agriculture. "There are rice paddies in China that have been producing for 4,000 years," he says. "There's no reason we can't do the same."

Once the grapes are harvested, the Chardonnay is pressed and the juice put in the stainless steel tanks to be chilled to about 50 degrees. Then it is barrel fermented and aged for about nine months. Red wines are fermented in stainless steel tanks as well. Wine is gently sprinkled over the "cap" to insure good contact with the skins. Following fermentation, the wine is put into combinations of French and American barrels, depending on the varietal wine. Mudd's passion is to create a really good bottle of wine that can be enjoyed in its youth.

Cinnabar annual Grape Stomp Festival

Only open a few times a year, a trip to the Cinnabar Winery is a treat. Tom Mudd and his team are knowledgeable and friendly, there's a great variety of wine, the mariachi band is usually playing, the barbecue is ready, and the view is magnificent.

Clos LaChance Winery

Clos LaChance Winery

1 Hummingbird Lane
San Martin, CA 95046
Phone: (408) 646-1050
Fax: (408) 646-1052
email: cheryl@clos.com
Web site:
www.closlachance.com
Annual Production: 5000 to 6000
cases
Winemaker: Stephen Tebb
Winery Owners: Bill and Brenda
Murphy

Access
Open weekdays 11-4;
  weekends 11-5

Tastings
$3 tasting fee;
Tour and tasting (call ahead): $10
per person
Wines: Chardonnay, Cabernet
Sauvignon, Merlot, Nebbiolo,
Pinot noir, Syrah, Zinfandel

Sales of wine-related items? Yes

Clos LaChance Wine Club
Two bottles eight times a year at
about $50 each shipment;
20% discount on shipments and
purchases at winery;
Invitations to additional events

Picnics and Programs
Picnic area;
Wine education events;
Event site for weddings, parties,
corporate events, winemaker
dinners and other events;
Participates in Santa Cruz
Mountains Winegrowers
Association events

The Clos LaChance Winery began in a garage in Saratoga and has grown into an old-world style facility with well-recognized wines. "Our goal," says Cheryl Murphy Durzy, marketing director, "is to make good wine that people like to drink."

In 1987 Bill and Brenda Murphy decided to put in a vineyard on their Saratoga property because they thought it would enhance the beauty of the land. The vineyard was such a success that they decided they'd make 50 to 70 cases of wine from their grapes as gifts for their friends.

Unfortunately, Mother Nature had other plans. In 1989 the Loma Prieta earthquake hit, destroying the Murphy's first vintage. The wine was ruined by the oxidation caused when the barrels were knocked over.

Ever resilient, they tried again and in 1992 delivered their first commercial vintage of 100 cases of Chardonnay. Clos LaChance Winery was born. The Murphys named their winery for Brenda's maiden name (LaChance) and a small fenced-in area encompassing a vineyard (Clos).

The pressure to develop more land for housing for nearby Silicon Valley employees decreased the amount of land for agriculture, including vineyards. To counteract this, the Murphys created CK Vines, a company that contracted with homeowners (like former figure skater Peggy Fleming) to put vines in their backyards in 1996. CK Vines managed the vineyard and purchased the grapes, giving Clos LaChance complete control over their fruit. This creative endeavor resulted in contracts with about 20 homeowners and vineyards ranging from 1/2 acre to five acres in size.

Like other start-ups, Clos LaChance didn't have an actual winery at first, but relied on Roudon-Smith, Savannah-Chanelle and the Novitiate to house their growing wine business.

Bill Murphy believes that it's best to "hire someone who knows how to do their job and let them do it," so they've relied on others to perform day-to-day winemaking and vineyard management. Still it is the Murphys who provide the vision for the style of Clos LaChance wines. Their aim is to have a stylistically and varietally consistent wine that goes well with food and is pleasant to drink.

In 1996 the Murphys felt that they needed to expand beyond their fabricated winery operation and move into a home of their own. Their small "estates" weren't producing enough estate wine. In a serendipitous connection, they met with the owners of the planned resort and golf course of CordeValle in San Martin. As part of CordeValle's commitment to the community, a certain portion of the land needed to be developed for agriculture -- specifically the traditional agriculture of the area -- grapevines.

Sunset over the Clos LaChance vineyard

The Murphys supervised the vineyard plantings and influenced the design of the 60,000-case winery building, incorporating gravity-flow technology and small-lot fermentation tanks. The result is a stunning Mediterranean style building in the center of many acres of vineyards. Driving down Hummingbird Lane, you can see the namesake birds, hawks and marsh birds, as well as the occasional fox. The Murphys chose the hummingbird as a symbol because they are the only beneficial bird in a vineyard; the rest will eat the grapes.

Like many small winemakers, the Murphys view wine as something that is integral to life, including its celebrations. Their vision for the winery included a facility that is available for corporate events and weddings. "Of course," Cheryl Murphy Durzy says, "people do have to understand that this is a working winery." She mentioned standing on the plaza watching a bridal car wend its way to the winery -- in the middle of a series of trucks bringing grapes to the crush pad for processing at harvest time!

Another important component of Clos LaChance is its education program. "Only 10% of people in the United States drink 90% of the wine," Cheryl says. Part of the reason is that wine appreciation remains a mystery to most people. Clos LaChance seeks to cultivate an understanding of wine in its consumers.

The Murphys begin in the tasting room with an essence table. The table is laid with several goblets containing elements that provide smells similar to those you might find in wine, for example, lemon, grass and toast. Since the nose is a critical factor of taste, the essence bar allows you to compare the elements you smell with what you taste in the wine. This enhances your vocabulary of wine.

The education extends to small group courses with such titles as "What a Difference a Glass Makes," "The Varietals of California," and "Winemaking 101." Clos LaChance's Director of Hospitality, Rick Toyota, is a genial and knowledgeable host at these events.

When all is said and done though, it's about the wine. Although an advocate for Santa Cruz Mountains' fruit, Clos LaChance also gets grapes from places that seem more suited to the particular varietal grape. For example, there is a Syrah from Paso Robles and a Zinfandel from El Dorado. The vineyard surrounding the winery in San Martin contains 22 different varieties -- the main Bordeaux grapes -- both red and white -- as well as red Rhône varieties. In addition, they have five clones of Zinfandel. Although still in its infancy, the vineyard promises a significant crop for future Clos LaChance wines.

The vineyards are managed in the safest way possible, although Clos LaChance isn't striving for an organic vineyard. Perhaps one of the more unusual aspects of the vineyard, besides its origin, is the use of technology to maintain the vineyard at an optimum level. Monitors throughout the vineyard check field and soil conditions. Computerized systems also measure and monitor the flow of water and fertilizers throughout the vineyard. This information is fed to computers in the winery so that the vineyard manager, Ben Scorsur, can take the appropriate actions. Bill Murphy's experience as a top executive in the tech industry has contributed to the impressive use of technology in the vineyard.

The Murphys acknowledge, however, that for all the gadgets and wizardry, grapes grow at their own pace, rather like children, and there's only so much control one has over the vineyard.

The people of Clos LaChance Winery consider the Santa Cruz Mountains one of the most important winegrowing regions in California. They invite you to visit to taste their wine, experience their tasting room and learn more about wine and its importance in life.

Rick Toyota hosting class on California Varietals

Fernwood Cellars

Matt Oetinger is one of the newer winemakers to join the Santa Cruz Mountains Winemakers Association, but he is not new to the wine business.

Matt's family homesteaded the property in the 1860s and still maintains a small ranch on the property run by Matt's mother, Linda Pond. At the turn of the century, a small group of cabins served as a retreat for San Francisco businessmen. Matt and his wife live in what was once the dining hall and common area for the retreat.

Fernwood cellar room

Redwood Retreat Road contains several well-known vineyards within the Santa Cruz Mountains AVA, such as Bates Ranch and Vanumanutagi Vineyards. In 1999 Matt also planted his vineyards on the road. He had served as "cheap labor" at his father's vineyard in Placerville and found he enjoyed the lifestyle, despite the hard work. Matt received a degree in biology from U.C. Davis and spent several years as the vineyard manager at Clos LaChance.

He credits the other wineries within the appellation for their contribution to his beginnings. "If I had to pay for consultation, I couldn't have done it," he says, naming people like Dave Gates from Ridge, Ben Meech, f.... and Marty Mathis from Kathryn Kennedy as particularly helpful to his vineyard debut.

The vineyard is planted using the Picchetti Zinfandel clone that Matt obtained from Ridge, as well as Cabernet Sauvignon, Syrah, Petite Syrah and Barbera vines. Matt believes that he needs to "bring the best fruit in the door and then stay out of its way." But, like an indulgent parent, he provides the best surroundings for the wine that he can. He includes the best yeast and cooperage he can find and custom designed a fermenter to insure that the cap stays submerged. Admitting that his winery is too small to make too many mistakes, Matt pays attention. He walks the line on filtering and fining wines, doing as little as he needs to, concentrating on keeping the character of a wine.

Ideally, Matt would like Fernwood wines to "surreptitiously become part of his consumer's lives," something that is associated with really special events.

The variety of the job keeps him going in this initial venture. The vineyards need work in the cool of autumn, winter and spring; the winery is a cool place during the heat of summer. The people he works with are friendly. He feels there's a chance to enjoy more good food, good music and art within the wine world, than in almost any other occupation.

Matt is passionate about his future as a winemaker and the future of the Santa Cruz winemakers in these mountains," he comments, "not just folks making wine in a tub."

With his vision and plans, Matt will soon be known as one of those real winemakers.

Fernwood Cellars

7137 Redwood Retreat Rd.
Gilroy, CA 95020
Phone/Fax: (408) 848-0611
Web site:
www.fernwoodcellars.com
Annual Production: 3000 cases projected
Winemaker: Matt Oetinger
Winery Owners: Matt and Tiffany Oetinger

Access
Open by appointment only

Tastings
No tasting fee
Wines: Cabernet Sauvignon, Syrah, Zinfandel

Sales of wine-related items? No

Picnics and Programs
Participates in Santa Cruz Mountains Winegrowers Association events

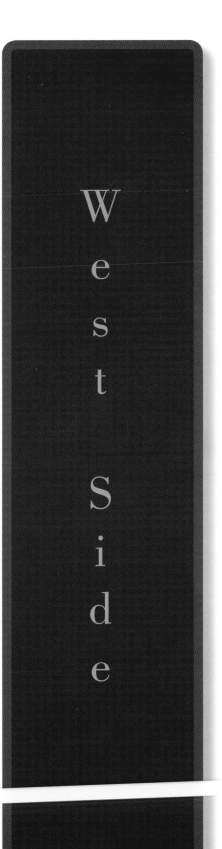

West Side

Obester Winery

Obester Winery

12341 San Mateo Rd.
Half Moon Bay, CA 94019
Phone: (650) 726-9463
email: info@obesterwinery.com
Web site:
www.obesterwinery.com
Annual Production: 2500 cases;
10,000 cases during bottling days
Winemaker: Kendyl Kellogg
Winery Owner: Kendyl Kellogg

Access
Open daily 10-5

Tastings
No tasting fee
Wines: Chardonnay, Sauvignon blanc, White Riesling, Champagne, Cabernet Sauvignon, Merlot, Sangiovese, port

Sales of wine-related items? Yes

Picnics and Programs
Picnic area;
Bottle and cork days;
Participates in Santa Cruz Mountains Winegrowers Association events

As different waves of winemakers went through the Santa Cruz Mountains, some wineries passed successfully from one hand to the next and some did not. Obester Winery has recently made the transition from its original owners and is poised on the cusp of creating new traditions, while keeping some of the old.

Obester Winery was founded by Paul and Sandra (Gemello) Obester in 1977. They were influenced by Sandy's grandfather, John Gemello, who came to live with them in 1974. Gemello had opened his own winery in Mountain View in 1934, and soon had his granddaughter and her husband making wine in their garage. The home winemaking lasted for two years, before the Obesters decided to go commercial and purchased the property at the edge of the picturesque San Mateo hills in Half Moon Bay.

The Obesters converted their barn into a winery and their car port into a tasting room. In 1989 they purchased land in the Anderson Valley region of Mendocino County and planted 45 acres of vines. The Gemello Winery in Mountain View continued operating under the direction of John's son Mario until it was relocated to Half Moon Bay in 1982.

The Obesters produced award-winning wine under both their label and the Gemello label. However, in 2001, after 25 years in the business, they decided they needed a change. At the same time Kendyl Kellogg wanted to leave a career in high-tech marketing and find something into which she could put her passion. The Obesters and Kendyl met, and the transition to new ownership began.

Kellogg felt instantly at home in an endeavor that blends the past and present. Living on the property gives her roots to the community, a community that includes both tourists just stopping by the winery for a casual visit, as well as "local wine zealots."

Obester Winery is home of the famed 'Bottle and Cork' days -- a madhouse of hundreds of people practicing a tradition that goes back to the winery's beginnings, and further past to the customs of many wineries in the early 1900s. The days occur about once a month and are a great way to buy high quality wine at a low price. Wisely, Kellogg decided to continue this tradition. On her first bottling day, the first bottle off the line was sold to Paul Obester.

Unwilling to merely own the winery, Kellogg decided to become the winemaker, too. Her initial training came from Paul Obester as well as from a few classes at UC Davis. "I find the industry incredibly collaborative," Kendyl says, "and my colleagues are ready to help when asked."

Entrance to the Obester Tasting Room

Life as a new winemaker wasn't always easy, however. Early in her career Kendyl needed to transport wine from Napa to Half Moon Bay. This required getting a wine tank to Napa. After many phone calls, she was told to "let her guys do it." "I am my guys," she replied. Undeterred she rented a truck, used a forklift to get the tank on the truck and delivered it to its destination in Napa.

Kendyl plans to produce three different labels, each representing a different "winemaker" from Obester Winery's history. Kellogg will produce a Cabernet Sauvignon and port bottled under her signature label. In addition she will continue to produce wine under the Gamello and Obester labels.

Luckily, she was able to inherit many of the Obester's relationships with viticulturists, but she remains particular about what she's looking for in a vineyard: well-kept vines, sanitation and a grower who is paying attention.

Kellogg doesn't believe that she'll begin growing grapes herself. "My strategy is to focus more on the retail side of the industry, making the winery a popular destination for travelers and Bay Area locals alike," she says. Her current production levels will probably remain the same, although she has plans to enhance the winery facilities.

Kendyl Kellogg's enthusiasm for her new life is still strong a year after her purchase. She loves the wine, the community, and people enjoying themselves. "It's such a great product," she says. Wine can join people and cultures together.

A short drive down Highway 92 from Highway 1 leads you past farms and pumpkin patches to Obester Winery. The winery is conveniently open seven days a week, with picnic tables available to enjoy your lunch with your wine. In addition to the normal wine-associated merchandise, Obester carries a line of gourmet foods. "Traditions continue at Obester Winery," Kellogg says, "but there are new traditions in the making."

As the generation that built the wineries in the 1970s moves on to another future, it is good to see that there are people willing to take up the dream that they began and carry it to the next generation.

"Bottle and Cork Day" at Obester

Bonny Doon Vineyard

Bonny Doon Vineyard

10 Pine Flat Rd.
Bonny Doon, CA 95060
Phone: (831) 425-4518
Web site:
www.bonnydoonvineyard.com
Annual Production: 250,000
cases
Winemaker: Randall Grahm
Winery Owners: Grahm family

Access
Open Daily 11-5 in Bonny Doon;
Tasting Room also available in
Paso Robles

Tastings
No tasting fee in Bonny Doon
$2.00 tasting fee in Paso Robles
Wines: Bonny Doon experiments
with many varietal wines and
blends, particularly Rhône
varieties (Marsanne, Roussanne,
Viognier), Grenache, Mourvèdre,
Cinsault, Carignan) and Italian
varietal wines (Barbera, Nebbiolo,
Sangiovese)

Sales of wine-related items? Yes

Distinctive Esoteric Wine Network (DEWN)
Two bottles of wine four or
six times a year (some wines
exclusive only to DEWN and not
available elsewhere)

Picnics and Programs
Picnic area;
Participates in Santa Cruz
Mountains Winegrowers
Association events

The city of Santa Cruz has an eclectic quality to it. The streets and mountains, beach and boardwalk provide a place where experimentation is welcomed. A free spirit drifts in the air, to be absorbed by any who are open to it. Randall Grahm, the owner and winemaker of Bonny Doon Vineyard, is open to it. According to Randall, Santa Cruz's "perverse

Randall Grahm

diversity of style" has developed his ability to play and experiment, leading to the creation and recreation of Bonny Doon wines.

The Grahm family bought property in Bonny Doon in the early 1980s. Around the same time Randall Grahm graduated from UC Davis with a degree in viticulture. Influenced by UC Davis research, and the success of the McHenrys and Ken Burnap with the Burgundian varietal grapes of Pinot noir and Chardonnay, Randall planted his vineyard with these grape vines. However, as he began to learn the winemaking trade and

develop his own style, he discovered his own palate was more suited to Rhône varietal wines like Syrah. In the late 1980s, Grahm began to graft and replant his vineyards over to the Roussanne, Marsanne and Syrah grapevines. By 1990, this transformation was complete.

Unbeknownst to Grahm, there was a silent stalker in Bonny Doon. He noticed that his vineyards displayed less vigor, but it wasn't until the neighboring McHenrys said that their vineyards had fallen victim to Pierce's Disease, that Grahm understood the demise of his own vineyard. By 1995 his vines were destroyed. Fortunately, Grahm had already purchased and planted vineyards near the correctional institution in Soledad, leading to the sobriquets used on his blended wines: Big House White and Big House Red.

The dedication to Rhône varietal wines was an uphill battle. These weren't grapes commonly found in California's wine regions. Grahm searched beyond California borders to obtain the grapes and quality he wants. Recently, more Rhône varietal grapevines have been planted within California and he can find what he wants closer to home.

At the same time that he was refining his winemaking style, Grahm also discovered the fun he could have marketing his wines. His labels (including work by Ralph Steadman) and marketing efforts are an art form unto themselves. Randall Grahm is the person you are most likely to find at wine events and written up publications beyond the environs of the Santa Cruz Mountains. Recently, Grahm says, he's "become emboldened, almost intoxicated with his power," particularly when it can be beneficial to advancing his beliefs.

To achieve the results he wants in a vineyard, Randall must frequently push beyond the comfort zone of the winegrower. Organic and sustainable vineyards are still a newer concept, but Grahm has the power to move his grape growers in that direction -- to "bring them into the 21st century." To do this, he needs to pay for the concepts that he embraces: lower yield, reduced or no irrigation, little or no pesticides, and enriched soil that has microbiological life.

Grahm has begun to expand beyond the Rhône varietal wines to the wines of Italy: Barbera, Nebbiolo, Sangiovese, and more. To aid in the development of Italian varietal wines, he has begun to explore the use of Old World vineyards and wineries to create his wines. Ever open to new ideas and experiences, Grahm is intrigued by the European approach to tasting wine. "When they taste the wine," he says, "they're very keen on the mineral aspects." He notes that they are looking for how the minerality reflects the *terroir* and texture of the wine. This is an aspect, he believes, to which Americans are largely color blind.

Experimentation and growth are hallmarks of Grahm's winemaking philosophy. "I want to make the most interesting, complex wines that are theoretically possible," he says. Initially, the grapes he had to work with for his Rhône varietal wines didn't always have the quality he was looking for. He had to pay attention to the blends and winemaker's craft to extract the flavor and structure he desired. He believes that the grape quality for these varieties is improving, and he will adjust his style to these changing conditions.

Grahm believes that his palate is more of a European or world palate, and less a straight fruit-forward Californian palate; this is the distinction that he brings to his wines. These are not "obvious" wines, Grahm says; they are designed for food and wine pairings. He avoids extremes such as too much tannin, too much oak, or too much alcohol. They are distinctive wines and blends that you are not likely to find elsewhere in the Santa Cruz Mountains, or even in most of California. However, Rhône varietal wines are beginning to emerge from the Bordeaux-Burgundy focus of California; as is evidenced by the popularity of the "Rhône Rangers" association. This group started in the 1980s and now consists of over 150 wineries from California, Idaho, Oregon and Washington.

Believing that his winemaking skills have brought the wines as far as that can go, Grahm is turning to the vineyard, searching for higher quality grapes. He wants to gain more recognition for his premium wines, as well as his more "light-hearted" vintages.

There is some difficulty with this prospect. Grahm has been such an excellent promoter of Bonny Doon wines -- his irreverent style and creative packaging have taken attention away from the quality of the wine he produces. As he moves into the future, he wants to see the perception of Bonny Doon change. He wants his wines to be known first for quality and then with a nod towards the equally creative publicity.

Grahm's original winery in the area of the Santa Cruz Mountains called Bonny Doon was a former saloon called the Lost Weekend. It now serves as the tasting room. There, beneath massive redwoods, you can experience the character of Bonny Doon wines. The present winery is in a former granola factory in Santa Cruz, not far from the Pelican Ranch tasting room. You might also catch a glimpse of Grahm as he travels about the city of Santa Cruz in his aging Citröen with the license plate declaring, "Cigare." Wherever he is, you can be sure that Grahm is continuing his quest for unique and unforgettable wines.

Bonny Doon Tasting Room

McHenry Winery

McHenry Winery

330 Eleventh St.
Davis, CA 95616
(Winery on Bonny Doon Rd.,
Bonny Doon, CA)
Phone: 530-756-3202
Web site: www.dcn.davis.ca.us/
~hmchenry/wine.htm
Email: lmchenry@dcn.davis.ca.us
Annual Production: between 300
and 400 cases
Winemaker: Henry McHenry
Winery Owners: Henry and Linda
McHenry

Access
Open by appointment only

Tastings
No tasting fee
Wine: Pinot noir

Sales of wine-related items? No

Picnics and Programs
Participates in Santa Cruz
Mountains Winegrowers
Association events

If you drive up Bonny Doon Road on one of the four Passport Days, watch for the small sign attached to the mailbox that announces McHenry Vineyards driveway. Turn through the trees and drive the dirt lane past the small vineyard. Park near the gray building nestled under a large redwood. Inside this rustic winery, Henry McHenry makes Pinot noir, and only Pinot noir. "Randall says you can't grow Pinot in Bonny Doon," Henry says, referring to Randall Grahm of Bonny Doon Winery. "I beg to differ."

An anthropology student at UC Davis, Henry fortuitously met his wife, Linda, in 1964. Fortuitously, because for a man who would eventually own a vineyard, it was nice to have a viticulturist in the family. Henry started teaching anthropology in Davis in 1971 and began making wine in 1975, although it was 1980 before the first commercial release.

The McHenrys lost their vineyard in 1993 due to Pierce's disease. Since that time, they have primarily used grapes from the Massaro vineyard in the Carneros District (south of Napa). The vineyard owners, Ray and Shirley Massaro, put aside a small plot of Pinot noir grapes especially for the McHenry's use, while the majority of their crop is used in Mumm's Napa sparkling wine. The McHenrys also purchased grapes from Amaya Ridge in the Santa Cruz Mountains.

In 1997 the McHenrys replanted their vineyard to Pinot noir: Pommard, Swan, Dijon 115 and Pinot noir 13 clones. In 2000, they were able to bottle their new 2000 estate Pinot noir.

Henry crushes and de-stems in an old Italian de-stemmer that, according to him, "is very gentle and exceedingly slow." He allows the grapes to ferment in small open containers and uses a non-native Wadenswil yeast. He ferments for about eight days, presses the must in an old basket press, and then finishes in 60 gallon French oak barrels.

Lots are small, but recognized. The 1997 Massaro Vineyard Pinot noir was one of 15 Special Recognition 4 Star Gold Medal awards at the Orange County Fair. Like many other wines from the Santa Cruz Mountains, McHenry wines have won recognition at the California State Fair, Los Angeles and Orange County State Fairs and the Santa Cruz Commercial Wine Competition.

A visit to the McHenrys is informal, and a warm sweater is advised. The winery dog may greet you; neighbors, and friends drop in to chat. Tasting is held in the barrel room of the winery. Henry stands in front of his Ken-Burnap-designed barrel racks. Bottles of Pinot noir stand on three barrels in front of the winemaker as he pours and carries on three or four conversations at once. Other barrels serve as tables for cheese and crackers. It's interesting to check the notes on the barrels, the dusty award ribbons and to discover the contents of the jug bottles at the ends of the racks. Linda McHenry takes the orders and Mrs. McHenry senior will often supervise the whole affair.

Henry, Jane, and Linda McHenry

Beauregard Vineyards

According to both Ryan and Jim Beauregard, owning a family winery has completely transformed their relationship as father and son. "We are good friends," Ryan says. His brother, Andre, is also part of the historical family business.

When Napoleon Bonaparte Beauregard left his native Quebec to settle in Boulder Creek, California, he probably didn't imagine that the next four generations of his family would become premium winegrowers in the region. Had he foreseen this, he would have been pleased. Napoleon's son, Dwight Amos, bought the Quistorf Ranch in Bonny Doon in 1945. The 125-acre Quistorf Ranch had been farmed since the time of the Homestead Act right after the Civil War. Records of Bargetto Winery grape purchases indicate that vineyards were present on the property in the 1930s and 1940s.

Dwight's son, Bud, took over the ranch from this father in 1961. Bud also purchased the Shopper's Corner grocery store in 1940. (Shopper's Corner carries one of the finest selections of Santa Cruz Mountains wines in the area.) The third generation of this winegrower family is Jim Beauregard. Jim, a strong proponent of the Ben Lomond Mountain AVA, says that the region is a more specific appellation and makes more sense than the broader AVA. "There are at least five different microclimates in the Santa Cruz Mountains AVA," he says, and of these, "Ben Lomond Mountain has 100% regional flavor." Jim believes that the consistent climate of the Ben Lomond Mountain area has been a significant factor in producing the best fruit and wine in the area for over a hundred years. In the 1970s Jim Beauregard also created a new company with an old name -- The Ben Lomond Wine Company.

After a brief foray in the winery business (see Hallcrest Winery), Jim concentrated on creating and maintaining vineyards both within Bonny Doon and beyond. He says, "Some people like golf or sailing; I like farming wine grapes."

Jim took over and remodeled the Quistorf [illegible] vineyards. The newest member of the family to enter the business, Ryan Beauregard, was born in the house in the center of the vineyard. Although it seems like a natural fit now, Ryan took a long detour before returning to the vineyard. Dropping out of high school and then getting his General Equivalency Degree (GED), Ryan attended junior college and studied winemaking at UC Davis Extension.

Ryan and Jim Beauregard

His first vintage, in the manner of many Santa Cruz Mountains winemakers, was created in his backyard, carport and living room in 1998. By 2000 he graduated to a custom crush arrangement with Hallcrest Vineyard.

Ryan's goals from this point are lofty, with an eye towards creating a premium wine from the premium grapes of his family's heritage. Jim Beauregard has plans to replant the old Locatelli property by Eagle Rock. Both Ryan and Jim believe that a winery is in the future, but economic factors at the end of 2003 are impeding the process. The heritage from these properties known for their quality wine for a century combined with the legacy, enthusiasm and talent of the Beauregard family indicate that it's only a matter of time before their premium wine gains wide recognition.

Beauregard Vineyards

P.O. Box 2809
Santa Cruz, CA 95063
Phone: (831) 425-7777
Fax: (831) 427-9468
email: ryan@benlomondmountain.com
Web site: www.beauregardvineyards.com
Annual Production: 4200+ cases
Winemaker: Ryan Beauregard
Winery Owners: Beauregard family

Access

No tasting room available
Wines: Chardonnay, Cabernet Sauvignon, Pinot noir, Late Harvest Zinfandel

Picnics and Programs

Participates in Santa Cruz Mountains Winegrowers Association events

Pelican Ranch Winery

402 Ingalls St.
Santa Cruz, CA 95061
Phone: (831) 426-6911
Web site: www.webwinery.com/
PelicanRanch
Annual Production: 1500 cases
Winemaker: Phil Crews
Winery Owners: Phil and Peggy
Crews

Access
Friday - Sunday 12-5

Tastings
No tasting fee
Wines: Chardonnay, Pinot noir,
Syrah, Zinfandel, Spectrum
Rouge (a Rhone-style blend)

Sales of wine-related items? Yes

The Pelican Ranch Wine Club
Two bottles four times a year at
about $45 each shipment;
Special event

Picnics and Programs
Participates in Santa Cruz
Mountains Winegrowers
Association events

Pelican Ranch Winery

Phil Crews is a joy to behold on Passport Saturdays. Flipchart in hand, hiking shorts and a t-shirt no matter what the weather, his enthusiasm for winemaking and education pours forth. Simple charts and apt questions draw you in and before you know it, you are expressing your opinions about the wines you are drinking – whether you think you understand wine or not.

As quickly becomes evident, Phil's "day job" is as an educator – a chemistry professor at UC Santa Cruz. He teaches periodic well-attended classes on wine chemistry and introduction to wine. His own education has been a product of hands-on learning and reading. "He has a large library," Phil's wife, Peggy, says. After all, Phil notes, most of the great winemakers of California learned from books, not classes.

His passion for home winemaking was so strong that when he proposed to Peggy, it was a "condition of marriage." He dreamed of his own winery, but work and children limited it to a hobby. However, kids have a way of growing, and so do hobbies, and in 1996 Phil found himself with a new relationship with both: "There were six barrels in the garage and three tons of grapes in the driveway." It was evident that either the hobby needed to scale back or it needed to go to the next level. And, according to Peggy, "Phil's not a scale-back kind of guy."

One of the benefits of living near the ocean is that it provides you with beaches for walking when you need to determine a course of action. Phil and Peggy took advantage of this benefit in August 1997 when they decided to create their own winery. They figured that they had barrels, fruit and a winery name, why not have a business?

The Roudon-Smith Winery gave them room to develop a winery under the Roudon-Smith bond in 1997. For the next five years, Phil developed his craft and style. It was also a time he used to develop relationships with vineyard owners, using contacts cultivated as a home winemaker, and then networking to be able to obtain high quality grapes. He also contacted past students to get to the right people: vintners who have a good reputation for producing quality fruit. Pelican Ranch wines are single vineyard designate, with grapes coming from the Santa Cruz Mountains AVA as well as others in central California: Dry Creek Valley, El Dorado, Los Carneros, Russian River and Santa Lucia Highlands.

Phil Crews

Phil Crews leading an experiment in wine tasting

Regarding his winemaking, Phil defines himself as a minimalist. "I collect lots of data," he says, "and then hope I don't have to use it." He goes on to say that a winemaker needs to make wine from the heart; science provides lots of theories, but there are too many buttons to try all the combinations. For example, he uses five different kinds of barrels, three different kinds of yeasts and separates the grapes by lots, even within the vineyard designation.

The wines are made in a Burgundy or Rhône style, depending on the grapes used. For Chardonnay he uses French barrels with 50% new wood each year. His barrel select is just that – these Chardonnays see 100% new wood each year. Phil is one of a few winemakers in the area who is using Oregon oak in his winemaking, obtaining barrels made in the French style at a Napa cooperage. All of his reds are unfiltered and unfined. The Chardonnays are both filtered and fined with egg whites.

Like most of the Santa Cruz Mountains vintners, Phil takes pride in his wines. But sometimes there are challenges. "The style of this appellation fits a Chablis style of Chardonnay; it doesn't have the buttery flavors." The Chablis style doesn't always resonate with

bottle is young. In fact, Pelican Ranch had a difficult time selling their 1997 Chardonnay when it was first released. A year later it was in high demand.

On March 28, 2003, the Crews opened their new winery and tasting room in Santa Cruz, two blocks off of Highway One in a newly developing area. They are next to Kelly's French Bakery – a great place for a snack to enjoy with your newly purchased Pelican Ranch wine. Peggy Crews runs the tasting room, a change from her day job as a speech pathologist. "I enjoy the social aspect," she says, although she also admits with a grin that there's been a learning curve working with Phil.

With a new business, there is no track record for sales, so it will take a year before they can gage the amount of wine they will actually sell at the tasting room. Phil says, "It's a do or die operation. If we don't make it, we'll have a ten-year supply of home wine." If they do make it, Phil will have other decisions to make. Right now, he's balancing winemaking, research, and teaching classes at UC Santa Cruz. "What do I give up?" he asks.

Only time will tell. In the meantime, be sure to stop by some Passport Saturday to hear Phil's lecture on different aspects of winemaking, tasting and storing wines. While they hope that you enjoy the high quality of their wines, Phil and Peggy also want to "send you away with something that you didn't know before" about wine.

Storrs Winery

Storrs Winery

Old Sash Mill
303 Potrero St. #35
Santa Cruz, CA 95060
Phone: (831) 458-5030
Fax: (831) 458-0464
email: winery@storrswine.com
Web site:
www.storrswine.com
Production: 10,000 cases
Winemakers: Steve Stores
Winery Owners: Steve and
Pamela Storrs

Access
Thursday - Monday 12 - 5

Tastings
No tasting fee
Tours available by appointment
only
Wines: Chardonnay,
Gewurztraminer, White Riesling,
Merlot, Petite Sirah, Pinot noir,
Zinfandel

Sales of wine-related items? No

Vin Express
Four bottles three to four times a
year;
Special events

Picnics and Programs
Participates in Santa Cruz
Mountains Winegrowers
Association events

If you stop at the Storrs tasting room, you'll see evidence that this is a family winery – a comfortable wicker chair, a box of books and a pail of Legos. Steve and Pamela Storrs' progeny, Aaron (born in 1994), Morgan (born in 1996) and Vianne (born 2002) are fully participating members of the winery -- picking grapes, attending trade shows and fighting over who gets to drive the forklift.

Storrs Winery

The Storrs are among the few winemakers in the Santa Cruz Mountains who actually planned and studied to make wine. They are devoted to creating the highest quality wine that they can possibly make, always searching to make the best better.

Encouraged by her grandfather to be the first woman in the family to graduate from college, Pam enrolled in UC Davis, eventually graduating with a degree in enology. Steve, who comes from a family who first arrived in the U.S. in 1664, studied viticulture.

Steve Storrs started his employment with Domaine Chandon and began to discover that he liked to make wine as much as grow the grapes. In 1980 he moved to Felton-Empire (now Hallcrest Vineyard) in Felton, California, where he worked as the red winemaker. Pam did her internship at Felton-Empire as well. In addition to their work for the winery, the two also found time to fall in love.

When she graduated in the 1980s, Pam became an enologist for the Almaden winery near Hollister, one of the largest barrel cellars in the world.

"Large wineries were generally open to women because they had a labor force and women didn't have to haul large barrels around. The smaller wineries could be a problem for women because they needed employees to do everything, but they didn't always have the equipment, like fork-lifts, to compensate. Today, many of the successful small wineries have grown a little bigger and they, too, have the equipment. It's easier for a woman to find a job in the smaller wineries today."

The Storrs began their life together in the winemaking business as consultants. Then they began Storrs Winery in the old Frick winery in 1988.

In the beginning they had no resources to buy land – even back then land in Santa Cruz County was pricey. But they did have relationships with the growers because of their previous work in the industry. They knew that they could get the grapes they wanted to make the handcrafted wine they hoped to produce.

The first two years that the winery was open, they shared the winemaking duties, producing 1500 cases annually in the beginning, growing to about to 10,000 cases annually. This is about where they want to stay in volume today.

"Spending time in the vineyards is my favorite activity," Pam Storrs says, "because great wine is made in the vineyards. And my favorite time in the vineyards is when the grapes are close to being ready." Pam and Steve are in every vineyard every other day during harvest season.

Steve and Pam Storrs

"In class," she adds, "they teach you that at a certain percentage of sugar and acid the grapes are ready, but I've found that isn't always true. I'll taste a grape and it's not quite there yet. I'll go back a day later and there's a very subtle movement in the sugar, but all of a sudden the grapes have their flavor and they are at full maturity."

Steve's goal in winemaking is to "express the character of the grapes in a particular vineyard." His hand-crafted wines are made in a hands-off fashion to bring out the various microclimates within the Santa Cruz Mountains. The winemaker's job is to take good care of the fruit, notes Steve. He keeps lots within the vineyard separate during fermentation and barreling, only blending lots of the same varietal wine from the same vineyard before bottling. Sometimes Steve will filter when he bottles. Fining the wine is sometimes necessary, but Steve but tries to avoid it. The winemaker tinkers with different yeasts and different barrel sources to fine tune the process. It's fascinating, Steve says, because "there's rebirth and regeneration of wine every year."

The Storrs have spent over a decade working with vineyard growers to get the vineyard management they believe is best for the wine. Steve also insures that the water content in the grapes doesn't dominate, so the flavor is there for him to bring out in the wine.

The whites are barreled in French oak, while the reds are barreled in a combination of French and American Oak. Steve pays close attention to the wines as they ferment, adjusting yeasts to produce the wines the Storrs prize.

The couple purchased 50 acres of land in Corralitos and moved there in 2002. The land is ideally suited to ripen grapes evenly, allowing the Storrs to harvest once, rather than block by block because of uneven ripening. This type of property can be difficult to find. Some of the properties, particularly if they have great views, are over exposed for grapes – the fog rolls in and it's too cool.

The Storrs believe that the Santa Cruz Mountains is poised to be one of the premium grape growing areas in California with high quality wineries. Because of the variety of microclimates, they believe there is an ideal place in the mountains for almost every varietal wine. They are passionate about the area and that's why they decided to raise their family and business here.

The couple has achieved several awards, including a Golden Bear award for Best of Show in the California State Fair's Commercial Wine Competition in 1994. The awards don't allow them rest, however, because their goal is to "make every single wine one of superior and unique quality -- wine with identity."

Storrs Tasting Room

Thunder Mountain Winery

P.O. Box 3969
Santa Cruz, CA 95063
Phone: (831) 439-8716
Fax: (831) 409-3334
email: tm@
  thundermountainwine.com
Web site:
www.thundermountainwine.com
Annual Production: 2000 to 4000
cases
Winemakers: Kira Maximovich,
Jon Cook
Winery Owners: Steve and Diane
Sterling, Sue Broadston, Kira
Maximovich, Jon Cook

Access
No tasting room available
Wines: Chardonnay, Cabernet
Franc, Cabernet Sauvignon, Pinot
noir, Syrah, Star Ruby (blend of
Cabernet Sauvignon, Cabernet
Franc and Merlot)

Sales of wine-related items? No

Club Thunder
1000 memberships for life; 5%
off shipments after purchase of
Thunder Box at $250.

Picnics and Programs
Participates in Santa Cruz
Mountains Winegrowers
Association events

Thunder Mountain Winery

Cult wines are difficult to define. There's a general stirring, whispers about fine wine and rumors about getting on a list to get on a list to get an allotment. If there are cult wines in the Santa Cruz Mountains, Thunder Mountain Winery definitely qualifies.

Milan Maximovich, a graduate student of Stanford University, was a chemistry student of Dave Bennion, one of Ridge Winery's founders. A germ of an idea began with that chance connection, because Milan began making wine in his cellar beginning with a 1977 vintage. Over the next few decades he learned his craft primarily by studying methods used in wines he admired the most: those from Bordeaux and Burgundy, France. "Milan didn't use the methods taught by UC Davis," his wife, Sue Broadston says. Instead he leaned more toward the classical French methods. This involved gentle handling of the grapes from the vineyard to the barrel, native yeasts, minimal racking, and no fining or filtration prior to bottling.

Early in his wine career, Milan came to believe that "single vineyard designation is the key to a distinctive wine." He claimed that preserving the individual character of the vineyard was as important as creating a high quality wine. This philosophy and Thunder Mountain's attention to detail are appreciated by most of the major wine reviewers, as Thunder Mountain receives consistently positive reviews and high ratings. You would have to look no further than the Santa Cruz Mountains vineyards of Bald Mountain and Bates Ranch to understand what Milan meant by "beauty in a wine glass."

In the early 1990s, Milan's stepson Scott Sterling suffered a car accident. Scott urged his stepfather to begin a winery, supporting it with funds from his settlement. Thus, in 1995, Thunder Mountain Winery was born.

From the beginning it was a family affair. Although Milan was the acknowledged winemaker, other members of the family took on supporting roles to get the winery running. The first few vintages were produced on a custom crush basis at Byington Winery and then moved to the current location of the Mirassou Winery on Aborn Street in San Jose. The entire family believed that Milan's palate and methods were good enough to produce wine capable of competing with the best from California.

Their daughter, Kira, began assisting Milan during the 2000 harvest in addition to working as a labor and delivery nurse. (Kira jokingly refers to the similarities between delivering babies and bottles of wine.) It was soon clear that she had inherited her father's palate and skill. In 2003, just before Milan Maximovich passed away, Kira took over as winemaker.

Kira Maximovich

Although Thunder Mountain wines can be difficult to find, the family attends frequent events both in the Santa Cruz Mountains and across the country. If you taste one of their wines, the family hopes that you will remember the "wow" that hit you with your first sip, and that you'll enjoy their wines for the rest of your life.

Clos Tita Winery

If you drive through France's wine country, you'll find many small vineyards owned by family winemakers. These winegrowers do it all -- maintain the vineyard, harvest the grapes and make the wine. This is the model for the Clos Tita Winery in Scotts Valley. With the sole help of his vineyard dog, Pablo, David Estrada runs the entire Clos Tita operation. "I make wine I like and if it sells, that's great," David says.

Estrada developed an appreciation for fine wines in the early 1970s. After a long day hunting quail in vineyards by the town of San Martin, David would join his friends at their family winery and enjoy different wines. In 1978 he began making his own wine as well as building his wine collection -- an optimum use in his mind for his UC San Francisco Dental School student loan.

of low-pruned vines, David prunes his Pinot noir grape vines (primarily Clone 15) using short canes, bilateral cordon, guyot or royette methods. The vineyard is dry-farmed with sustainable practices, such as hand hedging. Of course, he says, since his spacing is so tight, he doesn't have any other choice.

Because the vineyard is so small, Estrada obtains other grapes from Santa Cruz Mountain vineyards to complete his wine portfolio. These include Mount Eden district Cabernet Sauvignon; and Merlot and Syrah varietal grapes from Los Gatos.

In 1996 David's home winemaking venture turned professional and Clos Tita (based on his wife's first name -- Britta) was bonded. Although he is a "hands-on" winegrower, David is a "hands-off" winemaker whenever possible. The wine is fermented in small French oak barrels from premium coopers, with about 25-50% new wood each year. David doesn't filter or fine, believing that "some solids, if they are clean, enhance a wine's nose or mouth feel."

Clos Tita Winery

4 Kendall Lane
Santa Cruz, CA 95066
Phone/Fax: (831) 439-9235
Web site:
www.clos-tita.com
Production: 450 cases
Winemaker: David Estrada
Winery Owner: David Estrada

Access
No tasting room available
Wines: Cabernet Sauvignon,
Pinot noir, Syrah

Picnics and Programs
Participates in Santa Cruz
Mountains Winegrowers
Association events

David Estrada

David and his wife, Britta, purchased the Scotts Valley property in 1990 and began planting vines immediately. The plantings eventually took over the whole property, forcing Britta to move her horse elsewhere. (She breeds Hanoverian horses for dressage.) David moved the winery into the former stable.

The 700-vine vineyard is planted at a 900 foot elevation on a slope of 25 degrees. While the sandstone, the vines quickly run into the solid rock. David believes that the sandstone helps impart an earthy, complex mineral style to the wines. In keeping with the Burgundian tradition

David Estrada's goal is to produce small quantities of wines that will benefit from aging. To this effort he brings his dedication and patience, as well as strong beliefs in how to create the type of wine that he likes.

A hilltop in Scotts Valley can be a very different place from a hilltop in Burgundy. Yet, David Estrada has captured the essence of the Burgundian style of vines. There, within shouting distance of Silicon Valley, he can enjoy the fruits of his labor much like his French comrades.

Glenwood Oaks Winery

345 Neilson Ct.
San Jose, CA 95111
Phone: (831) 461-0668 or
 (408) 629-1188
Fax: (408) 629-2198
email: sales@
 glenwoodoakswinery.com
Web site:
www.glenwoodoakswinery.com
Annual Production: 2,000 to
4,000 cases
Winemaker: Val Rebhahn
Winery Owners: Val Rebhahn
and Thao Vinh

Access
Open Saturday 11-4:30
 at Roudon-Smith Winery
2364 Bean Creek Rd.
Scotts Valley, CA 95066

Tastings
No tasting fee
Wines: Chardonnay, Pinot noir,
Syrah

Sales of wine-related items? No

Picnics and Programs
Participates in Santa Cruz
Mountains Winegrowers
Association events

Glenwood Oaks Winery

If you visit winemakers in the Santa Cruz Mountains often enough, you'll hear them frequently talk about how supportive everyone is to each other, particularly when it comes to helping new wineries get started. Glenwood Oaks Winery credits their start to the generosity of the Roudon-Smith Winery which is where they make wine and provide their weekly tastings.

Like many winemakers in the mountains, Val Rehbahn didn't start out as a winemaker. In fact, he still has his day job at a Silicon Valley technical company.

Val Rebhahn

It all began in 1995 when Rehbahn's wife, Kit, decided it might be a lot of fun to plant grapes on their property. The property had been in the family for generations and had even contained grape vines. Those vines had been wiped out by phylloxera. So they started reading *Vines to Wine* and planned out their vineyard. In the meantime, Rehbahn enticed a fellow worker, Thao Vinh, to join in the project.

The Rehbahns planted the first string of Chardonnay grapes and decided it was fun. A second string went in and it was still fun. Then they decided to plant the rest of the acreage. Rehbahn, the engineer, determined that it would take 823 vines to finish the job, so they obtained dormant, bare root grapes from a nursery. The weather turned warm and the vines started to wake up in the bags and needed immediate planting. Suddenly, it wasn't fun anymore.

Fortunately for the Rehbahns, they had good neighbors. "Mike and Peggy Sullivan saved us," Val says. They got 18-20 Mormon kids to help plant and the vines made it into the ground. However, they still had no irrigation and no trellising.

The trellising search took them to Napa. There, they were once more stumped when the man asked them, "What kind of trellising would you like?" Val said, "We don't know. What would you suggest?" With more valuable help, they arrived home with materials for trellising and drip irrigation. That problem solved, they moved on to the next project of every Santa Cruz Mountains winemaker -- a fence to keep out the deer.

About this time Thao suggested that there was a better margin in producing wine than in merely selling grapes. Excited, they went to their friends at the Roudon-Smith Winery with flipcharts in hand and began to describe their business plan to create a winery.

When they were done, Bob Roudon pointed out that making wine was easy, but they'd have to sell it. In their eagerness, Val and Thao proposed buying a winery. Roudon suggested that they learn how to make wine first and after two years he'd see if they were serious. The subsequent conversation, which took place in August of 1997, went something like this.

Val: What do we need to make wine?
Bob: Grapes.
Val: What else?
Bob: Barrels.
Thao (to Val): You go get the grapes and I'll get the barrels. (to Bob) What kind of barrels?

Bob explained the kind of barrels they should purchase and recommended Chardonnay grapes. Val began to call people to get grapes since their home vineyard wasn't ready for harvest. He arranged with a Central Valley broker to get ten tons of Chardonnay and a ton of Merlot. The broker sent his driver north, suggesting an alternate route to avoid the weigh stations. Unfortunately, the driver missed a turn and found himself at a weigh station with an overloaded truck. Three hours later, the broker called Val who went to Gilroy with pitchforks, bins and a pickup truck to unload the Merlot.

Back at the winery, the conversation continued:
Bob: Where did you get those grapes?
Val: The valley
Bob: I can see that.
Val, after a silence: Think we can make wine?
Bob: We'll see.

They crushed and pressed the grapes, learning the process on the way. During a winter tasting, Val checked in with Bob, "How do you think the wine is?"

"We'll see," came the reply.

At the end of June the wine was bottled. Val again asked Bob, "What do you think about the wine?"

"I think we have something here," Bob replied.

Excited by his new venture, Val took his wine to the Santa Cruz County Fair and won a commercial silver medal. He told Bob. Bob said, "If you enter enough contests, you will get a medal, you know," before smiling to let Val know he was joking.

In subsequent years, Val has begun to harvest his own Chardonnay grapes and has found more consistent grape sources for the other types of wine he makes: Pinot noir and Syrah. He continues to pursue his goal to become a full-time winemaker. His only regret is that his wife, Kit, didn't live to see the winery's growth. She died in April of 2002.

"She was proud of what we'd done," Val says. She remains his inspiration and in her honor, he has renamed their Vinh-Rebhahn Vineyard in Glenwood "Kit's Vineyard."

Susanne C...   ...event

Bargetto Winery

Bargetto Winery

3535 North Main St.
Soquel, CA 95073
Phone: (831) 475-2258
Fax: (831) 475-2665
email:
customerservice@bargetto.com
Web site:
www.bargetto.com
Annual Production: 40,000 cases
Winemaker: Paul Wofford
Winery Owners: Bargetto Family

Access
Soquel
   Open Monday - Saturday 11-5
            Sunday 12-5
Monterey (700 L Cannery Row)
   Open Daily 10:30 - 6

Tastings
No tasting fee
Tours available by appointment
only
Wines: Chardonnay,
Gewurztraminer, Pinot grigio,
Carignan, Dolcetto, Cabernet
Sauvignon, Merlot, Pinot noir,
Zinfandel, Melange (white blend),
La Vita (blend of Italian red
varietal wines), sparkling wine,
mead, olallieberry and raspberry
dessert wines

Sales of wine-related items? Yes

Bargetto Wine Clubs
Monthly Club: two bottles of wine
per month
Quarterly Club: six bottles of wine
four times a year
Chaucer's Club: three bottles of
dessert wines four times a year

Picnics and Programs
Picnic area; Event site for small
weddings, parties, winemaker
dinners and other events; Art
gallery;
Participates in Santa Cruz
Mountains Winegrowers
Association events

Bargetto is the oldest winery in the Santa Cruz Mountains, as well as the third largest winery. It was born after the demise of Prohibition in 1933, when two Italian brothers, John and Philip Bargetto, started selling their wine to the Santa Cruz community. At that time their holdings were four acres near the center of the town of Soquel and a 52-acre ranch nearby.

Philip died in 1936, leaving John responsible for the family business. John continued, with the help of his sons, Lawrence and Ralph, and Philip's daughters, Sylvia and Adeline, to establish the winery. Barrels were the medium of exchange during these early years; they were carted down to local restaurants and the Bargetto's store on Water Street in Santa Cruz where the wine sold for 25 to 50 cents per gallon. In 1948 the Bargettos sold the 52-acre ranch and began to depend entirely on purchased grapes from various Santa Cruz Mountains growers. In spite of this cost-cutting move, the brothers found that they could not support both their families. By mutual agreement, Lawrence took over the business in 1963 from both Ralph and his father, John; running it until his unexpected death in December 1982. Today, Lawrence's wife, Beverly, and their children run the business.

Paul Wofford

During the early 1980s, Lawrence was the primary winemaker, assisted by his son, John, but in 1986 Paul Wofford joined the firm and took over that position. The family made another significant move in 1992. They purchased 50 acres near Corralitos and planted 40 acres of it with Chardonnay, Merlot, Pinot noir and Italian varietal grapevines including Pinot grigio and Dolcetto. This area, called Regan Vineyard, provides the Bargettos with quality mountain fruit for their wine. John Bargetto calls Regan Vineyard the most important thing that the family has done in the last 10 years. He says, "It's allowed us to expand the number of wines produced and the number of Santa Cruz Mountains' varietals."

In addition to his work as winemaker at Bargetto, Paul Wofford is a well-known wine consultant on the west side of the mountains. Like many winemakers of his generation, he didn't intentionally pursue the trade; his college degree was in geology. "I discovered that there weren't many jobs in the field in the 1970s," he says. Returning to school, he took classes in enology and began his training at small wineries such as Clos du Val and Zeca Mesa.

Paul stays with Bargetto because he values the winery's history and dedication of the family. "The international headquarters is at grandma's house," he says. Despite the close-knit nature of the family business, Paul maintains autonomy in his work. The location of the winery is also appealing. During the spring, he takes his lunch to the porch and watches the steelhead salmon spawning in Soquel Creek.

A look at the rock patterns surrounding the creek will tell you that it's not always peaceful, however. In the years 1955-56 and 1982, the river flooded, coming up between the floorboards of the deck overhanging the creek. Tree trunks and logs that were carried by the swift current also threatened the winery building, but it survived in both cases -- only to be threatened by another show of nature's violence.

The 1989 Loma Prieta earthquake brought barrels of Nebbiolo crashing to the floor. The door to a fermentation tank of Chenin blanc opened as well, dumping the entire tank of wine down the drain. As with the economic cycle, the Bargettos took it in stride and continued onward.

Today the scene is calmer and the direction more focused. Another winemaker influenced by Martin Ray, Paul Wofford holds that the winemaker is the caretaker and that wines, do, in a sense, make themselves. He believes in minimal cellar intervention, but insures that his wines get the treatment that they need. This can mean different yeast strains, barrels, fining, micro-oxygenation, filtering, or a dozen other slight corrections that the winemaker can incorporate. He knows that he must treat the wines like individuals, not applying the same techniques to all.

machine might be running or there could be the frenzy of harvest. Yet, there's an unmistakable sense of tradition, of doing things the way they have been done for over 70 years.

Within the tasting room and adjacent patio, you can appreciate local artwork as you taste the different varietal wines that Bargetto produces. According to John Bargetto, the winery produces more Santa Cruz Mountains wine than any other area winery. Bargetto's is known for its quality control from the vineyard to the marketplace. The last decade has seen an appreciation of their Italian heritage, leading to a refocus on these varietal wines. "We're growing varietals that have never been grown in this area," says John. "It's kind of fun." The ultimate

Jesus Aceves and Roberto Gutierrez pruning in Bargetto's Regan Vineyard

Under the Chaucer's brand, Bargetto Winery is known for their dessert wines -- raspberry, olallieberry and mead. (Mead is a sweet wine made from honey.) In fact, they are the number one producer of mead in the country. However, as Paul points out, the fruit wines may open the door, but the varietal wines need to be taken seriously in order for the winery's reputation to prosper. We have "a broad range of very good wines to appease almost all types of wine people," Paul says.

winery, particularly during the week. The doors to the old barn are open and cellar workers keep busy, moving barrels, boxes and other mysterious pieces of equipment. The bottling

expression of this is their relatively new release of an old blend -- La Vita. Because they believe in the interconnection of wine and art, they will change the label of La Vita each year to display an important piece of art in which wine has been portrayed.

Bargetto Winery, close to the heart of Soquel, is a neighborhood winery with many return visitors who come by to pick up something for the evening meal, just as people used to bring their jugs to the Bargetto winery. As you taste their wine, remember the hopes and dreams of two brothers from Italy who bequeathed their legacy through three generations.

Hunter Hill
Vineyard and Winery

7099 Glen Haven Road
Soquel, CA 95073
Phone: (831) 465-9294
Fax: (831) 475-5060
email: christine@
hunterhillwines.com
Web site:
www.hunterhillwines.com
Annual Production: 2400 cases
Winemaker: Vann Slatter
Winery Owners: Vann and
Christine Slatter

Access
Open June-Sept
Saturday and Sunday 11-4;
Oct-May Saturday 11-3
or by appointment

Tastings
No tasting fee
Tours available by appointment
only
Wines: Merlot, Pinot noir,
Syrah, Zinfandel, Hunter's Blend
(Cabernet Sauvignon, Merlot,
Syrah)

Sales of wine-related items? No

Picnics and Programs
Picnic area, including views of
The Forest of Nisene Marks State
Park and the Monterey Bay;
Participates in Santa Cruz
Mountains Winegrowers
Association events

Hunter Hill
Vineyard and Winery

As you drive up the hill, you know that the view will be stunning. Turning into the driveway, you sense the welcome will be warm. If it's Passport Day, you can smell the tri-tip cooking. You park your car, gaze at the vineyards and listen to the starlings and finches telling the news of the day. Through the winery door, Christine and Vann welcome you to taste the fruits of their labor.

"It's one more thing we get to do together," Vann says as he smiles at his wife of 38 years.

In the late 1800s, the Manildi family settled in the Santa Cruz Mountains, developing a fruit orchard with apples, cherries, plums and wine grapes. Wine was made for home consumption and to provide drink for field workers. They were given a bottle of wine at lunch and a bottle at dinner -- a common practice in the Santa Cruz Mountains.

As a matter of course, the Manildis had children and eventually grandchildren. One of these grandchildren, Christine, married Vann Slatter and they returned to the original homestead to raise their own children (then 6 months and 3 years old). It was supposed to be a temporary haven, but 35 years later, they are still here.

Hunter Hill Tasting Room

In the early 1990s, the apple trees that were on the land weren't doing very well. In a land use decision, the Slatters pulled out the trees and planted the area with vines. Since Merlot was what they drank, Merlot was primarily what they planted. The first 300 vines were planted in 1992 and Vann began to make wine. He took classes from Paul Wofford, winemaker at Bargetto. His family loved his wine, and so did all his friends.

The Slatters second set of vines went in a few years later, yielding a vineyard planted with Merlot, Cabernet Franc and Syrah. In 1998 the winery moved from the basement to the newly built winery and Hunter Hill was bonded. Like many Santa Cruz winemakers, Vann buys other people's grapes to round out his selection of red wines. This process has enabled the Slatters to develop strong relationships with vineyard owners in other locations, including Bob Schulenburg in Lodi and Gard and Lori Hellenthal near Cazadero. They value these friendships as much as the award-winning wines they get to create from these grapes.

While Hunter Hill might seem like a natural name for the winery that belongs to a couple that enjoys duck hunting, the winery did come dangerously close to being called Chicken Hill Winery. However, Father Scott, their parish priest, convinced them that naming the winery after their dog, Hunter, was a better choice. So Hunter, the dog, went on the winery labels. When you visit the winery, be sure to ask to see the image of Hunter on the tasting bar.

Christine and Vann Slatter

Vann tends his vineyard in a semi-organic manner, using organic practices as much as possible. Like most winemakers, he picks his fruit by taste, but also insures that sugar and acid are at the desired levels. Because Hunter Hill only produces red wines, the processing is simpler. Grapes are de-stemmed and put as whole berries directly into one ton vats. There the grapes ferment for five to seven days and are punched down gently with a wooden punch three to four times every 24 hours before they are pressed and put into French and American barrels. Vann uses 50% new barrels each year. Wines are held one to two years in the barrel, depending on the variety. Vann occasionally fines, but doesn't filter, his wines.

He's methodical in his practices. "We're a small winery and we only get one chance at it." He pays close attention to the barreled wine, determining exactly when to bottle.

Hunter Hill produces an estate Merlot and is in the process of creating an estate Syrah. They also produce an old vine Zinfandel, using grapes from 40-year-old vines in the Schulenburg Vineyard.

Vann feels the winery is just about at the right size; they won't grow much bigger than they are. Hunter Hill plans to continue to focus on premium wines and grapes from the Santa Cruz Mountains area. "This area is passed over all the time," Vann says. "The Santa Cruz Mountains will come into their own soon." He added that the history in this area is amazing, with vineyards dating back to the 1800s.

The tasting room is small, but you will receive a warm welcome at the redwood tasting bar. The room also serves as the production room of Hunter Hill; you might be surrounded by barrels, or have the opportunity to watch Vann test his wine. On either side of the tasting bar are murals done by Lynda Dann, picturing new grape vines and vegetables. If it's Passport Day, the open air kitchen behind the tasting room will be fired up for tri-tip steak. "It's our son's secret recipe," says Christine. "He won't tell anyone."

The Slatters have strong ties to the land they live on. "I walk through the vines," Christine

riding on a plow horse over this same ground when she was eight years old."

"We never take it for granted," Vann adds. From the tasting room window you can see the redwoods of the Forest of Nisene Marks State Park. As you walk out the door of the tasting room you are surrounded by grape vines.

The Slatters want to share the enjoyment in the land and the fun of making and drinking wine with you. They encourage you to bring a picnic lunch to have in the gazebo so you can surround yourself with good food, good friends, good wine and good scenery.

And, Vann says it's O.K. to walk through the vines.

Hunter Hill Vineyard

Soquel Vineyards

Soquel Vineyards

8063 Glen Haven Rd.
Soquel, CA 95073
Phone: (831) 462-9045
Web site:
www.soquelvineyards.com
Production: 2000 cases
Winemakers: Paul Bargetto and
Jon Morgan
Winery Owners: Peter Bargetto,
Paul Bargetto, Jon Morgan

Access
Saturday 10:30 - 4:00

Tastings
Wines: Chardonnay, Cabernet
Sauvignon, Pinot noir, Trinity
(blend of Cabernet Sauvignon,
Carignan and Zinfandel)

Sales of wine-related items? No

Wine Club
Two bottles of wine every two
months for about $45 a shipment;
Annual event

Picnics and Programs
Participates in Santa Cruz
Mountains Winegrowers
Association events

Soquel Vineyards is at the top of Glen Haven Road in Soquel and is one of the few places in the area that is convenient to two other wineries. You can begin your day with wine tasting at the Bargetto Winery, continue to Hunter Hill and finish with another branch of the Bargetto family at Soquel Vineyards.

Peter and Paul Bargetto, who own the winery along with partner Jon Morgan, are descendents of John Bargetto, founder of Bargetto Winery down the hill. John had two sons, Ralph and Lawrence; Peter and Paul are Ralph's twin sons. The piece of land on which their new winery sits also has historical significance because the 5.29 acres are part of the 52-acre ranch that the Bargetto family acquired in 1919 and subsequently sold in 1948.

Peter and Paul Bargetto opened Soquel Vineyards a short distance down the hill from their present location in 1987. They leased that property, but continued to search for a permanent home. Drawn to their grandfather's former land, Peter and Paul knocked on the door of a house located on the property. Turned down by the owners, they continued looking. However, a short while later, the owner suffered a stroke and couldn't maintain the holding anymore. The former owners felt it was fitting that the Bargettos have the right to buy it and the property was sold to them in 1999. Paul now lives in the house on the property with his family.

The brothers have created a small boutique winery with a limited quantity of carefully structured wines, focusing on fruit from the Santa Cruz Mountains. Having no grapes of their own, they still managed to acquire historic mountain fruit. Since 1987 they have purchased some of their grapes from the Peter Martin Ray Vineyard. (Peter is the adopted son of Martin Ray and his vineyard is on the remnant of property left to Ray after his conflict with the Mt. Eden group.[1]) Their wine is also made from grapes obtained from other vineyards in the mountains. In addition, they purchase grapes picked from 120-year-old vines in Lodi to make their Zinfandel.

The Bargettos have built an elegant winery, using roof tiles from a 1751 farmhouse in Lucca, Italy. The side door to the winery is made from a recycled 12,000 gallon Bargetto Winery redwood wine tank, originally made from virgin redwood that is about 1300 years old. The doors weigh 300 pounds each and it took Jon Morgan 150 hours per door to make them. Morgan says, "Never again!"

Virgin Redwood Door

The tasting room is light and airy, with a view of the bay. Paul's son, Michael, made the tasting bar as part of his senior project in high school. Well beyond the bird house stage of carpentry, the bar top is composed of rich redwood and mahogany. Outside the French doors, rich grass invites you to take off your shoes and walk. A running fountain lulls your senses as tension and the cares of the daily life fade.

The brothers are planting Pinot noir and Nebbiolo on the property. Also in the plans is the creation of olive oil from the 60 olive trees they've planted on the property. So far they've managed to can some olives. They hope to get two gallons of olive oil after the current harvest.

Soquel Vineyards raises the term "hand-crafted" to new levels. The vineyards with which they contract generally dry farm, producing smaller berries with rich intense flavors. Because of the cool nights and warm days, there's a longer hang time for the grapes before they reach the sugar content that the Bargettos want for their grapes.

Once they bring back the few tons of grapes, they (and sometimes a few of their friends) dump the Chardonnay grapes into the wine press and press the grapes by hand. The juice is put into a stainless steel tank for four to five days before being racked off and put into French oak barrels for 44-45 days of fermentation. They are then aged for eight to nine months.

The Pinot noir grapes are fermented with their skins for about 15 days before going through the same dumping and hand pressing ritual, although they bypass the steel tank. The same is true for the Cabernet Sauvignon grapes, although they ferment for an average of 23 to 30 days on the skins. The Pinot noir is aged for nine to ten months; the Cabernet Sauvignon is aged for 24 to 30 months.

Soquel Vineyards is destined to remain a boutique winery as there are no plans to scale up in quantity. Instead, the brothers want to concentrate on improving their wines -- the common goal of many fine winemakers in the Santa Cruz Mountains. After all, as Peter Bargetto says, "if you are going to pay $20 to $50 for a bottle of wine, it had better be a great one."

The views from the winery are worth the drive up the mountain to the site located 1015 feet above sea level. With the bay spread out in front of you, it's easy to understand the Bargetto's passion to reclaim their history. The tasting room experience almost always includes a barrel sample; watching Peter or Paul clamber among the barrels makes you feel part of the winemaking experience. A guided tour around the property to admire the view, current projects

Barrel tasting at Soquel

and the burgeoning olive trees may also be included in the visit. "People have a great time here," Paul says. "They relax in the calm and quiet." He also notes that by the time they leave they almost always join the wine club. This is probably good, since the bulk of the winery's sales are to their wine club members and visitors.

The owners of Soquel Vineyards hope that you will recapture this relaxed mood when you open a bottle of Soquel wine: the view, the artistry of the winery, the history and the quality. "It's all part of the experience of the wine," Peter says.

(Footnotes)
[1] See History for more detail

Aptos Vineyard

Aptos Vineyard

7278 Mesa Dr.
Aptos, CA 95003
Phone: (831) 688-3856
Fax: (831) 662-9102
Annual Production: 400 cases
Winemaker: John Shumacher
Winery Owners: Patti and John Marlo

Access
No tasting room available
Wines: Chardonnay, Pinot noir

Retired Superior Court Judge John Marlo

"The thing I like about vines," retired Superior Court Judge John Marlo says as he looks across his vineyard to the Monterey Bay, "is that they do what you tell them. While a defendant often goes right when you tell him or her to go left," he adds, "a vine goes in the direction you prune it."

Although John directs the vine canes, the original concept for the vineyard came from his wife, Patricia. She thought it would be nice to look over vineyards towards the bay. Patti came from a ranching family and believed the grape harvest would bring their family together every year, just like roundup does for ranchers.

They planted 1,000 Pinot noir vines with the help of friends one morning early in the 1970s, using the 10 foot by 8 foot spacing popular at the time. Despite the fact that the county agricultural department predicted that the vines would never thrive so close to the ocean, the vineyard provides an average of two tons of grapes per year. "It's a lot of work," John says, "but it's good therapy."

John isn't the winemaker for the Aptos Vineyard wines; instead he relies on other winemakers within the Santa Cruz Mountains Winegrowers Association. However, if you believe as many winemakers do that the wine begins in the vineyard, Aptos Vineyard wines have been successful. They have won numerous awards in the Orange County Fair, a prestigious annual wine event near Los Angeles.

The vineyard isn't included the Santa Cruz Mountains AVA; it's 200 feet too low in elevation. "I should have lobbied harder," John says ruefully, referring to the development of the AVA in the early 1980s.

The Marlos harvested their last viable crop from the Aptos Vineyard in 1996. The vines were hit with a bacterium similar to Pierce's Disease and have since been replanted. You'll find a "Judge's Reserve" Chardonnay in the stores, but the grapes haven't come from this vineyard, but from other vineyards in the Santa Cruz Mountains. Soon, however, the vineyard will be back to producing fine Pinot noir grapes and Aptos Vineyard's award-winning wine will be available again.

Once the grapes are ready, Patti will recreate the annual family event. The Marlo family (five children, eight grandchildren and one great-grandchild) will be back to harvest grapes and enjoy a barbecue.

Salamandre Wine Cellars

Wells Shoemaker's passion for winemaking began when he visited Italy at the age of nineteen. He had a Fiat 600 and a large-scale map of Tuscany with dotted lines marking roads. He'd find a dotted line and "drive that little old tin can car to the end; there was always someone making wine at the end of the dotted line." The Italian home winemaker at the end of the road would inevitably want to know how Wells got there and if he was hungry. "It was only 20 years after the war and Americans hadn't quite worn out their welcome," Wells noted.

Back in California, Wells finished his training as a pediatrician and moved to Aptos which in 1975 was known only for the endangered Santa Cruz long-toed salamander. As he began to realize his passion to make wine, the salamanders climbed all over the barrels that he had stored under and behind his house. When the winery was bonded in 1985, Salamandre seemed like a natural name. Stuffed, clay and glass replicas of the amphibians keep him company as he makes his rounds on the barrels.

Wells was drawn to winemaking not only to drink the fruit of his labors, but to embrace the lifestyle. Reminiscing about his trip to Tuscany, he says that drinking wine in Italy in the 1960s was the polar opposite to drinking in California. In Tuscany, "if you got drunk, you were a hopeless dweeb, a man not to be trusted." There was tremendous peer pressure not to get drunk in Italy, a much healthier culture. Wine was part of the meal and there were many, many generations of modeling the integration of wine with life.

Another reason Wells wanted to incorporate wine into his lifestyle was that he admired how in Tuscany, the "culture of winemaking was one of great reverence for the land. If there was an olive tree with one sprout left, people would protect it." In California growling machines gnawed out orchards and vineyards in storms of dust and noise to create Silicon Valley.

Like many vintners, Wells rhapsodizes about spending time in the vineyards, particularly as harvest approaches. He doesn't own his own grape vines, but purchases fruit from vineyards in the Arroyo Seco area.

In 1996 Wells Shoemaker chose quality over quantity when he reduced his volume to preserve the results he wants. Along with fewer cases of wine, Wells is now producing more red wines than whites.

He and his wife, Sandie, like the flexibility of winemaking. Harvesting and bottling are the only tasks that demand their immediate attention. Everything else can be scheduled around taking care of their family. However, sometimes they have to decline extended family obligations. But, as Wells points out with a shrug and a wink, "It's the head of the household's obligation to make the wine."

The Shoemakers also enjoy the customers and friends they've developed over the years in the winemaking business. Wine is a celebration of life, another day lived. "You're alive here for another dinner," Wells says.

Wells Shoemaker at Salamandre Open House

Salamandre Wine Cellars

108 Don Carlos Dr.
Aptos, CA 95003
Phone: (831) 685-0321
Fax: (831) 685-1860
email: newt@cruzio.com
Web site:
www.salamandrewine.com
Production: 1200- 1500 cases
Winemaker: Wells Shoemaker
Winery Owners: Wells and Sandie Shoemaker

Access
Open by appointment only

Tastings
No tasting fee
Wines: Chardonnay, Merlot, Pinot noir, Primativo, Red Table Wine (Merlot, Primativo, Syrah)

Sales of wine-related items? No

Picnics and Programs
Participates in some Santa Cruz Mountains Winegrowers Association events

Trout Gulch Vineyards

414 Avalon Ave.
Santa Cruz, CA 95060
Phone: (831) 471-2705
email: gerry@
   troutgulchvineyards.com
Web site:
www.troutgulchvineyards.com
Annual Production: currently less
than 1000 cases
Winemakers: Gerry Turgeon,
Bernie Turgeon and Paul Wofford
Winery Owners: Gerry and
Bernie Turgeon

Access
No tasting room available
Wines: Chardonnay, Pinot noir,
small lots of sparkling wines

Sales of wine-related items? No

Picnics and Programs
Participates in Santa Cruz
Mountains Winegrowers
Association events

Trout Gulch Vineyards

Gerry Turgeon is the passionate winemaker of Trout Gulch Vineyards. Gerry and his father, Bernie Turgeon planted vineyards with Jerry Lohr in the 1970s. They were part of Turgeon and Lohr Winery until 1984 when they sold their shares and the winery became J. Lohr Winery.

Gerry then went into the microbrewery business in Santa Cruz, forming the Santa Cruz Brewing Company and the Front Street Pub with his dad. In 1987 they planted about 25 acres of vineyards, primarily Chardonnay with a few rows of Pinot noir, in the town of Aptos within the Santa Cruz Mountains. Gerry says, "It was an extended garden; a place where Dad could maintain a healthy connection with the land."

Gerry Turgeon

The first vintage was created using the custom crush facilities at Bargetto, as well as the consultation help of Paul Wofford, the Bargetto's winemaker. It was released in 1988. Since then, they have produced between 600 and 2200 cases annually. In 1995 they had a small harvest generating less than 300 cases of Chardonnay that won Gold Medal, "Best of Bay Area Varietals" and "Best Chardonnay in the State" awards at the California State Fair Wine Competition. In addition, Gerry has discovered that the complexity of their clones coupled with the *terroir*, climate and other conditions has made Trout Gulch "perhaps one of the best sites for Pinot noir on the planet!"

Gerry worked the vineyard, made the wine, and handled the marketing for Trout Gulch Vineyards during the late 1990s by himself. But in 2000 the floor dropped on grape prices. "I had 25 tons of Chardonnay still hanging and unsold in October of that year."

As a result, Turgeon, *Pere et Fils* (father and son) sold the vineyard to their neighbor, although Gerry still contracts to obtain the grapes. About the same time, the Bargetto's Regan Vineyard production came online and the Bargettos needed the room at their winery for the new source of grapes. That year Gerry moved his winemaking operation to a "state of the art winery" in Hollister.

As winemakers, Gerry believes that Paul Wofford, his father and he are stewards of the wine. "The only reason to mess with wine is if it needs it," he says. Occasionally, they'll do a light fining, and they will pre-filter before bottling. Gerry Turgeon's primary goal is to develop a many-layered wine which he believes is accomplished 90 % in the vineyard with only 10 % done in the winery.

Although there is no Trout Gulch tasting room, you can taste the wines at many of the Santa Cruz Mountains Winegrowers Association events, as well as in many local restaurants.

The flavor of a Trout Gulch Wine should be, according to Gerry: "Time in the bottle; a time capsule that portrays a remembrance of everything that occurred over the entire vintage in the little postage stamp of a vineyard in the mountains.

Windy Oaks Estate Vineyards and Winery

From the crest of the Windy Oaks Vineyard, you can see past Bargetto's Regan Vineyard, over the alluvial plain to the Monterey Bay. A thousand feet above this plain, two old California oaks guard the crest, inspiring the name of the vineyards and winery. Behind you is the bulk of the vineyard, divided into blocks with such names as Middle Kingdom Block and Redwood Grove Block. The vines are trim and the trellising tight. You know this is a winery that pays attention to detail.

Judy and Jim Schultz

Judy and Jim Schultze came home to California in 1994 after business took them to many parts of the winery world, including the Yarra Valley in Australia and a stint in London that gave them easy access to the vineyards of France, Italy and Spain. After determining that the land they had purchased in Corralitos was well-suited for Pinot noir grapes, the Schultzes' primary focus became the Burgundy region of France.

They planted their first three acres of Pinot noir in 1996, and since have added 11 more acres of Pinot noir and one acre of Chardonnay vines. The vineyard is maintained as close to organic as possible. They recycle the grape must into the vineyard, and rotate the cover crop, but also use

great deal of attention to canopy management, pruning to insure only two shoots per spur, and insuring cordons are properly trellised and the leaves are adequately thinned.

This attention to detail continues to be a focus through harvest. Although they check brix, acid and other statistics, Jim says, "Numbers don't tell you a thing." Instead, they rely on daily visits to the vineyard, examining seeds and stems and tasting grapes to get the result that they want.

Their winemaking process is Burgundian in tradition and totally hands on -- the only pumps they use are to clean hoses. Using a custom built machine, the grapes are sorted so that only the finest go into the crusher-de-stemmer. After an extended cold soak, the Schultzes put the grapes in half ton open bins and hand punch every three to four hours. "It's like feeding a newborn," Judy says.

The Pinot noir goes through extended maceration and then is barrel aged in French oak for 18 to 24 months. The Chardonnay is aged *sur lees* for 12 months. Both wines are aged in the bottle before release to eliminate bottle shock as much as possible.

While this is the general process, Jim admits that every year is different and paying attention to annual differences yields greater quality.

Although newcomers to the business -- their winery was bonded in 2001 -- the Schultzes are passionate about the vineyard, the wine and the Santa Cruz Mountains AVA. They remind people that Wine Spectator has called this appellation the most underrated appellation in the world. Other owners and winemakers in the area have helped them get started by loaning them equipment and advice. Both Schultzes love spending time in the vineyard, working with the earth and creating wines that have a lot of structure and age well. They are thrilled to create a wine that brings great satisfaction to the people who drink it.

Windy Oaks Estate Vineyards and Winery

380 Sweetwood Way
Corralitos, CA 95076
Phone: (831) 786-9463
Fax: (831) 724-9577
email: proprietor@
   windyoaksestate.com
Web site:
www.windyoaksestate.com
Annual Production: 1000 cases
Winemaker: Jim Schultz
Winery Owners: Judy and Jim Schultz

Access
Open by appointment only

Tastings
Wines: Chardonnay, Pinot noir

Sales of wine-related items? No

Windy Oaks Estate Wine Club
Special offers and information

Picnics and Programs
Participates in Santa Cruz Mountains Winegrowers Association events

River Run Vintners

65 Rogge Lane
Watsonville, CA 95076
Phone/Fax: (831) 726-3112
email: riverrun@cruzio.com
Web site:
www.riverrunvintners.com
Annual Production: 1000 to 3000 cases
Winemaker: J.P. Pauloski
Winery Owners: J.P. and Kris Pauloski

Access
Open by appointment only

Tastings
No tasting fee
Wines: Chardonnay, Carignan, Cabernet Sauvignon, Malbec, Syrah, Zinfandel and whatever else the vintner is in the frame of mind to make

River Run Vintners Wine Club
Two bottles three times a year

Sales of wine-related items? No

Picnics and Programs
Participates in Santa Cruz Mountains Winegrowers Association events

River Run Vintners

At River Run Vintners time seems to stand still. During a Passport Saturday, winemaker J.P. Pauloski presides over a table of seven or eight different types of wines and talks about wine with the people who visit.

"Thirty years ago I really wanted to brew beer, but then I found out it cost a quarter of a million dollars to start a brewery," J.P. quips. Ten years of making beer and cider finally evolved into winemaking.

Once he decided to make wine, he built a cellar into the hillside under his house in Santa Cruz and began to pursue his craft. During the 1970s he was a professional river guide and was naturally attracted to a bottle of River Run Zinfandel at a gathering.

A year later he bought River Run Winery.

vineyard or parts of the same vineyard year after year. His favorite time of year is about a month before harvest, when some saner creature is hiding nuts in a tree. "I like to get up at some ungodly hour and circulate the vineyards and talk to the people there." A self-described "kinesthetic kind of guy," you can almost imagine him feeling the grapes, trying to determine how best to preserve the fruit of the grape in the bottle.

The transformation the wine goes through between the grape and the bottle fascinates J.P. This transformation includes the hands-on tasks of crushing and punching down red wine. The process frequently results in the "purple-hand look." He's gone to seminars where winemakers state that they don't like to cook. "How can you make wine if you don't like to cook?" he asks, "It's an elemental skill."

J.P. is known for small lots of a great many varietal wines. When he feels that he can do a new wine, and he has the space and money to do it, he'll try it out. With love he'll nurture the

J.P. Pauloski (sitting behind table) on a Passport weekend

Although the primary reason for buying the property was to buy the house, J.P. was happy to have the winery as well. J.P and his wife, Kris, took over the River Run bond that had been established in 1978, although the government took about eight months to approve them. The day after the bond was approved, nine tons of Zinfandel grapes rolled down the driveway and J.P. was in business.

J.P. has spent a lot of time building relationships with growers, using the same

fruit into the bottle, resulting in a taste that uniquely describes the varietal wine grape.

Once he's done that, he enjoys sharing his wine with the customers that come to his winery, discussing wine in general and hearing their reactions to his creations. So take a Saturday to drive down to the southern end of the Santa Cruz Mountains Winegrowers Association, wander through J.P's wines, taste the hors d'oeuvres that Kris makes, and perhaps watch a lazy hawk fly overhead. You won't regret the trip.

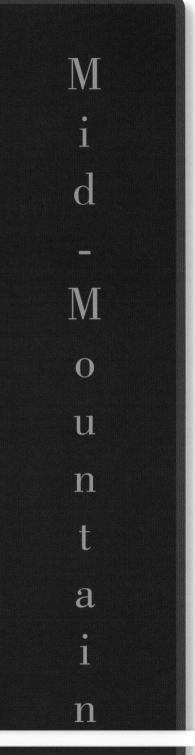

Mid-Mountains

Hallcrest Vineyards/ Organic Wine Works

379 Felton-Empire Rd.
Felton, CA 95018
Phone (Hallcrest): (831) 335-4441
Phone (OWW): (800) OWW-WINE
Web site:
www.webwinery.com/hallcrest
www.webwinery.com/OWW/
Production (Hallcrest): 5,000 cases
Production (OWW): 10,000 cases
Winemaker: John C. Schumacher
Winery Owners: John, Lorraine and Shirin Schumacher

Access
Daily 11-5:30
Tours available by appointment only; small fee applies

Tastings
Hallcrest Wines: Chardonnay, Cabernet Sauvignon, Syrah
OWW Wines: Chardonnay, Carignan, Pinot noir, Syrah, A Notre Terre (blend), Radical Red (blend)

Sales of wine-related items? Yes

Picnics and Programs
Picnic area
Participates in Santa Cruz Mountains Winegrowers Association events

Hallcrest Vineyards/ Organic Wine Works

John Schumacher is passionate about organic wine. Always a front-runner in this philosophy, his winery was the first to offer 100 % organically processed wine in the United States. However, as his wife, Lorraine Schumacher, points out, "We want you to drink our wines because they're good, not because they are organic."

The vineyard was not organic prior to the Schumacher's purchase of the property. The Hallcrest Vineyard is actually one of the older vineyards and wineries in the mountains, although there were times in its history when the winery did little more than gather cobwebs from overactive spiders.

Chaffee E. Hall, a San Francisco lawyer, established Hallcrest in 1941 at a 40-acre site adjacent to his family's summer home in Felton. With the help of Manuel Silvey and a strong horse, he planted 15 acres of his land with Cabernet Sauvignon and white Riesling, using a St. George rootstock. The first few vintages were made by Herman Wente, but Hall began making wine in 1946 after the winery building was built.

In 1956 Hall's daughter, Marie, and her husband, Penry Griffiths, took over most of the winery tasks. They'd migrated from horse to jeep, but still were doing most of the work themselves. However, by 1964 they decided to retire and began selling the grapes to Jim Beauregard, and then a succession of other wineries. The winery sat unused until Leo McClosky, a biochemist

Spring Lupines at Hallcrest

from Ridge, Jim Beauregard and John Pollard, an airplane pilot, decided to start a winery. They purchased the 10 acres of white Riesling vines and the winery from the Griffiths in 1980 and called their winery Felton-Empire. For seven years they created wine, before over-expansion caused them to sell. The Schumachers purchased the winery in 1987.

John got his start in winemaking at age 13 by picking and fermenting the family plums while his parents were on vacation. While the first result wasn't what he hoped for, he knew what he wanted to do. As soon as high school was finished, he enrolled in the enology department at UC Davis. In 1984 he and Lorraine started their first winery in their garage. When the opportunity came to move to Felton and expand the winery, they jumped on it -- not only to give the winery more room, but also to have a place to raise their family so they would have an appreciation of living on the land. The Schumachers believe the winery business is something that they can hand down to their three children. They approached Marie Griffiths about restoring the Hallcrest name and permission was gratefully granted.

John went to work transforming the vineyard maintenance to organic methods, developing the first certified organic vineyard in central California in 1989. While many wineries use organically grown grapes, John has gone a step further and developed wines that are organically processed as well.

One of the differentiators between John's organic wine and other organic wines is the lack of sulfites (SO_2) in OWW wine. Sulfites are added during the winemaking process to prevent oxidation and unwanted organisms that can spoil wine. They are added during the creation of many food processes as well. Some people are sensitive to sulfite, leaving them with stuffy noses and asthma-like symptoms.

John believes that extreme cleanliness and temperature monitoring can prevent these problems as well as sulfites can, with an added benefit to the wine consumer. As a result, his OWW wines have minimal or no sulfite in them. Schumacher is only one of two wineries in the entire country with an organic, unsulfited wine with national distribution. His was first winery to release 100 percent certified organic wines in the United States.

Ironically, California is one of the more difficult places to sell organic wine. Organic wines received a reputation for poor taste about a decade ago and that reputation has been difficult to live down. In addition, the cult of wine focuses on wines designed to age, as in the big Cabernet Sauvignons of Napa. The wines that John makes are drinkable without aging, and they are flavorful as well.

For the Hallcrest label, John concentrates on making wines that are distinct to the source of the grapes. He's constantly asking the question, "What's the style we want to bring out of the appellation?" To this end, the Hallcrest style is evolving.

John deliberately keeps his production down. In addition to making wine, Hallcrest provides "custom crush" facilities. Many of the small wineries in the mountains without a winery facility take advantage of John's hospitality. The winemaker obtains the grapes, crushes and ferments them at Hallcrest, and leaves John and his assistant, Kenny, with a list of instructions.

The guest winemaker makes frequent contact with the Schumachers, as well as periodically "visiting" his or her emerging wine. John provides a great deal of knowledge to the fledgling winemakers in the mountains.

John believes that the Santa Cruz Mountains are a great appellation: diverse, with "secretive hidden treasures," providing a remote and small style of living. "It's not a fanfare region," Lorraine says. The people are close in spirit, if not close in miles, as was demonstrated during the 1989 earthquake. However, the Schumachers suspect that there is a lot of potential in the mountains that isn't being realized. Instead of trying to duplicate Napa with a different source of grapes, they need to focus on wines that reflect the appellation. As a result, John is also beginning to focus on Pinot noir, the grape of strife for many in the mountains.

The Schumachers believe that their organic processes bring them closer to a sense of community with people who have sensitivity to sulfites, as well as the community in their home town. They provide donations to local programs, but also rejoice in the fact that people who couldn't drink wine before, can finally taste the wine product of the Santa Cruz Mountains.

Hallcrest tasting room

Cordon Creek

Cordon Creek

Phone: (408) 292-6252 or
(831) 588-2056
Fax: (408) 295-2629
email: rbiringer@
cordoncreek.com or
mattb@cordoncreek.com
Web site:
www.cordoncreek.com
Annual Production: 900-1000
cases
Winemakers: Roger Biringer and
Matt Buchanan
Winery Owners: Roger Biringer
and Matt Buchanan

Access
No tasting room available
Wines: Sauvignon blanc,
Cabernet Sauvignon, Syrah,
Syrah blush, Zinfandel, Late
Harvest Zinfandel, Meritage (red
blend)

Wine Clubs
Two bottles four times a year

Picnics and Programs
Participates in Santa Cruz
Mountains Winegrowers
Association events

Matt Buchanan and Roger Biringer want to take their small lots of wine beyond technical measurements and the winemaking craft to a place that reflects the artistic nature of the process and the taste of the palate. Matt and Roger first met as student and teacher in a biochemistry class at San Jose State University (SJSU).

Roger received his PhD. in biochemistry from UC Santa Cruz in 1985 and began teaching at SJSU in 1987. Nine years later when Matt graduated with a degree in microbiology, the pair made a pact to produce their first vintage as home winemakers by the end of 1996. They obtained grapes for a Cabernet Sauvignon, Zinfandel and white Riesling and entered amateur wine events with their results. Several ribbons at tasting events enticed them to enter the world of commercial winemaking. Cordon Creek was bonded in 1997.

The grapes used by Cordon Creek for Cabernet Sauvignon, Sauvignon blanc, Zinfandel and Syrah come from several vineyards in El Dorado and Amador counties. The choices of growers are based on location -- including weather, soil, elevation and the like -- as well as the character of the vineyard owner. Matt and Roger look for someone to produce grapes in a manner that appeals to them, including how the grower prunes and how long the vines have been producing. Included in their search are vineyards within the Santa Cruz Mountains AVA.

Roger and Matt pick their grapes a little riper than most winemakers and are willing to pay the price for alcohol levels above 14% to produce the wine they envision. (The government levies an extra tax for wine with alcohol levels higher than 14 %.) A custom crush arrangement with Hallcrest provides them a place to make their wine.

Their concentration at this point is on reds, including a Meritage blend; however, they also produce a good Sauvignon blanc. The Sauvignon blanc is barrel fermented in neutral American oak after crush. Roger and Matt add yeast to the barrels and use a *sur lees* process to produce a richer wine.

Matt Buchanan and Roger Biringer plan to make Cordon Creek a sustainable winery over the next decade, reaching an annual production of 10,000 cases. In the meantime, they will continue to create hand-crafted wines that reflect the *terroir* where the grapes are grown.

Photo courtesy of Cordon Creek Winery

Matt Buchanan

Photo courtesy of Cordon Creek Winery

Roger Biringer

Andersen Vineyard

According to Alan Andersen, owner and winemaker at Andersen Vineyard, the wine heritage in the Andersen family is strong. In 19th century Copenhagen, his forebears were wine merchants. You could say it's in his blood.

The family heritage bloomed again in the 1950s when Alan's family purchased acreage above Felton. In the 1960s they planted 22 1/2 acres of Cabernet Sauvignon, Pinot noir, Syrah and Chardonnay, primarily using their neighbor's land, with a small section of vines on their own property. Unfortunately, the fates were against them. Within a few short years blight hit the vines at the same time an irrigation gear broke in 110-degree heat. The vineyards went downhill from there. After that, Alan studied jewelry design, developed a jewelry business and started his own family. In the late 1980s Alan moved his business (Andersen Jewelry Design) to Felton and began to restore the family vineyard by attacking the berry bushes that had taken over.

In 1989 he completed his move back to the Felton area and planted five acres of Cabernet Sauvignon (75%) and Merlot (25%) using phylloxera-resistant rootstock. Alan is dedicated to organic farming as described by the 1990 Organic Food Act, but hasn't applied for certification because it's too expensive.

Alan's winemaking and jewelry craftsmanship are deeply intertwined. He creates custom jewelry, particularly wedding rings and other symbols of friendship and love. "I craft something carefully from thought and imagination," he says. He brings this same art to his vineyard and winemaking.

After the intense work of jewelry making, it's almost a relief for Alan to tend his vines. Like many small winemakers, he says, "it's a lot of work and good exercise, too." But he finds the lifestyle and the attention he can bring to his winemaking rewarding. The winemaking life is a natural, quality life -- and it's all about family. "My elderly parents [almost 90] live on the property." His son, Ian, now a student at California Polytechnic Institute, minors in viticulture and helps Alan when he can. Alan takes an old-fashioned pride in his work, providing a slow but steady attention to the vines and winemaking.

Alan's signature wine, Romantic Red, is a Bordeaux blend of Cabernet Sauvignon and Merlot. Andersen works hard to get the fruit to ripen with a long enough hang time to develop the richness he seeks. But he also pays attention to the weather. Heat and rain are not always the same from year to year. Because his vineyard is just below the peak of a small mountain overlooking Zayante Canyon, the microclimate is different from that of other parts of the mountains.

Alan Anderson pouring at "Wine with Heart"

This focus on detail for a single blend produces a wine that Alan Andersen believes will add pleasure to the quality of your life -- particularly special celebrations with friends, or romantic moments for two.

Andersen Vineyard

P.O. Box 1117
Felton, CA 95018
Phone: (831) 336-3525
Fax: (831) 336-3005
email: alan@
AndersenVineyards.com
Web site:
www.andersenvineyards.com
Annual Production: 300 cases
Winemaker: Alan Andersen
Winery Owner: Alan Andersen

Access
No tasting room available
Wines: Cabernet Sauvignon, Merlot, Romantic Red (blend)

Equinox

290 Igo Way
Boulder Creek, CA 95006
Phone: (831) 338-2646
Fax: (831) 338-8307
email: info@equinoxwines.com
Web site: www.equinoxwine.com
Annual Production: 500-600
cases
Winemaker: Barry Jackson
Winery Owners: Barry and
Jennifer Jackson

Access
Open by appointment only

Tastings
No tasting fee
Wines: champagne

Sales of wine-related items? No

Picnics and Programs
Participates in Santa Cruz
Mountains Winegrowers
Association events

Equinox

Barry Jackson

Champagne intrigues Barry Jackson, owner and winemaker of Equinox. "There's no money in it," he confesses, "but it is the road less traveled." This is particularly true in the Santa Cruz Mountains, where Equinox is the only winery that makes sparkling wines their main offering.

A California native, Barry has been in the wine business since 1974. In 1979 he began working at the Paul Masson Winery in Saratoga. Paul Masson began production of Santa Cruz Mountains' champagne in 1896, carrying the product through Prohibition as "medicinal champagne." Working at the historic winery gave Jackson the education and passion to make what he calls the "ultimate food wine."

Leaving Masson in 1985, he worked for Seitz, a wine equipment manufacturer, for two years before founding his own wine consulting establishment, Harmony Wine Company, in 1987. The consulting business gave him the stability and flexibility he needed to think seriously about establishing Equinox.

Unfortunately, Barry picked a less than optimum time to begin his endeavor -- October 1989. His first batch of juice was fermenting in the Storrs Winery when the Loma Prieta earthquake hit on October 17th. Moments later it was raining Chardonnay inside the winery. Jackson lost half his product, but not his determination.

The process of making champagne is a long one. While Jackson, like many winemakers, focuses on the fruit in the vineyard, he acknowledges that the time to pick grapes for champagne is different from the time most winemakers pick grapes for still wines. Jackson says the reaction of most winemakers is "You're going to make wine from that?" He adds that the grapes from the Santa Cruz Mountains are a great source of the balanced yet tart flavors he's looking for. The climate is similar to that of Champagne, France -- a cool growing area.

The second component that Jackson focuses on for fine champagne includes sound winemaking practices and good barrels. He believes that there's more to winemaking than chemistry and claims, "the more you know the more you know how to and how not to do things based on the book." Of course, he adds that how you want things to turn out and how they actually do turn out are not always the same.

The wines are barrel-fermented in well-seasoned barrels: Jackson isn't looking for wood flavors in his champagne. "My wines are on the stylistic fringe," he says. "Very dry with a good viscosity to the base wine which gives it a better mouth feel."

After barrel-fermentation, the wine is bottle-fermented with extended (*tirage*) aging on the yeast for years -- six or ten, depending on the style -- before disgorging and storing "on cork" for another period of time. To get an idea of how long this process takes, the 1995 vintage was released in 2001.

Jackson believes that "wine is the entertainment factor of food," and hopes that his consumers will remember that they really enjoyed his sparkling wines. He finds that there is something special about champagne that creates interesting anecdotes and is always intrigued when someone sends him a note that begins, "I drank your wine and..."

Ahlgren Vineyard

Ahlgren Vineyard

20320 Highway 9
Boulder Creek, CA 95006
Phone: 800-338-6071
Fax: 831-338-9111
Web site:
www.ahlgrenvineyard.com
Annual Production: 2,500 to
3,000 cases
Winemaker: Dexter Ahlgren
Winery Owners: Dexter and Val
Ahlgren

Access
Open Saturdays 12-4

Tastings
No tasting fee
Wines: Chardonnay, Semillon,
Merlot, Cabernet Franc, Zinfandel,
Cabernet Sauvignon, Nebbiolo,
Syrah

Sales of wine-related items?
Limited

Ahlgren Wine Club
Shipments two times a year;
10% discount on bottles at winery;
15% discount on cases

Picnics and Programs
Beautiful views; call ahead to
reserve small table in the garden
or picnic table for larger parties

Participates in Santa Cruz
Mountains Winegrowers
Association events

Ahlgren Vineyard began under a kitchen table in Sunnyvale, California in the late 1960s. Val Ahlgren started the family's winemaking career creating fruit wines. Within a few years, Dexter Ahlgren, a Silicon Valley civil engineer, became interested in her hobby. Before long they found themselves crushing two tons of grapes in their driveway and storing their wine in French barrels in the garage turned wine cellar.

The Ahlgrens soon realized that making wine in a growing Silicon Valley bedroom community was not going to be a long-term prospect. In 1971 they began their one-year search for a piece of property with a southern exposure and room for their future wine business and home. Dexter sold his interest in a small engineering firm and became an independent consultant, thus gaining the ability to work wherever he wanted as long as he could have access to his clients.

The property they found is nestled seven miles north of Boulder Creek with views of the surrounding mountains. At 1100 feet above sea level, the climate is cool, yet above the summer fog line. The land had been clear cut and stumped in the late 1800s, so the Ahlgrens were free to begin building. "It's a lovely place to live," Val says, not too close to neighbors, surrounded by watershed, and just the right size for a small family winery.

The Ahlgren's first commercial crush on their new property was in 1976. They produced 900 gallons of wine with grapes from the Bates Ranch, Monterey Ventana and Sonoma Chauvet vineyards. By that time, Dexter had taken over as winemaker with Val working as cellar master. According to Val, Dexter has the palate, the nose, and a good sense of intuition.

The Ahlgren Barrel Room

Because their vineyard is small (one acre), the bulk of their grapes continue to come from other vineyards. They've continued their relationships with Bates Ranch and Monterey Ventana and developed new ones with growers whom they regard as exceptional grape producers. The Ahlgrens prefer to develop wines that are associated with a particular vineyard, rather than "dumping the grapes all together." As a result, Val notes, they are writing the history of those vineyards.

While many of their vineyard relationship are within the Santa Cruz Mountains AVA, the Ahlgrens have a strong affiliation with Livermore Valley Vineyard for Zinfandel and Semillon grapes. They were first introduced to the Semillon grape in 1979 when the managers of the Semillon block within the Novitiate vineyard offered to sell them grapes. In 1981, however, they needed to find another source because that year the Novitiate crop was lost to cutworms. Val and Dexter turned to Livermore Valley,

Springtime at the Ahlgren Vineyard

convinced that it was and is a great place for the variety, given the valley's gravelly soils. Happy with the result, they've made Semillon from Livermore grapes ever since.

As winemaker, Dexter feels that the "wine wants to make itself – just squeeze the grape." Consequently, he uses a hands-off approach, sometimes using wild yeast, but primarily inoculating the musts with a pure strain of wine yeast. Other than the Semillon, he inoculates his wines for malolactic fermentation. Ahlgren's white wines are generally filtered and fined, but he rarely fines and never filters the reds.

Like many wineries, the Ahlgrens are heavily invested in their barrels. They buy quality oak barrels and do all the fermenting of whites in them. The reds are fermented in open top containers to allow hand punching of the caps. Barrels are replaced on a five year program with 20% new barrels each year. Dexter prefers the Chardonnay in French oak and the Semillon in American oak.

There is a lot of labor involved, although that has eased a bit since they've "moved one step past the Neanderthal wine making stage" with the recent purchase of some top-notch equipment that allows for high quality handling of the grapes with less back-breaking labor. Dexter has an assistant winemaker, a necessity since his stroke a few years ago. ("Dexter was the only thing that wasn't Y2K compatible," Val quips.) They also hire local labor to help crush and bottle.

The Ahlgrens replanted their steep one acre vineyard with two-year-old dormant field grown rootstock and field grafted Pinot noir clones in the summer of 2002. Choosing the Pinot noir grape came after some trial and error – they hadn't realized how cool their property was. After some unsuccessful tries of Cabernet Sauvignon and Merlot, they settled on the Pinot noir, despite the fact that it's a "fussy grape." In 2003 the Greyhound Run Vineyard (named after their rescued racing greyhound, Willie, who passed away in 2002) will produce its first estate grown grapes. "After all," Dexter said, "we *are* a vineyard."

drew Val and Dexter from their respective careers of teacher and engineer. For them, the best part of winemaking is the ability to live where they do and enjoy the company of others who enjoy wine. "Wine brings people together," Val said. "There's no political or religious discussion," Dexter added, "just talk about good wine."

The Ahlgrens find people involved in the wine business to be part of the joy. They are friends with the restaurateurs in the area. "They're young, vibrant and a lot of fun." And, as well, the Ahlgrens have fun with the people that come to taste their wine on Saturdays, the members of their wine club and those that show up for special events, such as a library wine tasting and annual cellar sale.

At their age, Dexter and Val face the fact that they, like so many of their contemporaries in the Santa Cruz Mountains, will need to move on sooner than they'd like. So far, none of their children or grandchildren appears to want to take on the family business, but that can't be ruled out. They do believe, however, that there's a new generation of winemakers in the mountains and the legacy they have built will live on.

In the meantime, drive up Highway 9 some Saturday, past the deer fence gate and a quarter mile up the gravel driveway. Take time to admire the redwood house, Val's garden, the jewel of a vineyard, the madrone and redwood trees. Be sure to play with Art, the big French poodle. Dexter will be waiting for you under the market umbrella, ready to present his latest creation.

Dexter Ahlgren

P•M Staiger

Although only 20 minutes from downtown Boulder Creek, Paul and Marjorie Staiger could be in another world. Their five-acre vineyard, winery and house perch on the side of a mountain, giving them a dramatic view of the folds and peaks of the Santa Cruz Mountains.

About 35 years ago, when Paul began his job as an art instructor at San Jose State University, the Staigers began to make wine. They had a small house on a hill in Los Gatos at the time, and began their winemaking careers by toting a quarter of a ton of Zinfandel grapes up 65 steps to crush. In spite of the effort, they were hooked.

In 1970 they leased the Los Gatos Novitiate vineyard with a group of friends. The group also obtained a bond at that time so they could legally make the amount of wine that they wanted to make, although none of the wine was ever sold commercially.

Paul and Marjorie decided that they wanted to have a vineyard and winery of their own, but they wanted it to be manageable. "We don't want to think of this as work," Paul says. They asked Brother William from the Novitiate how many acres two people could reasonably tend. The answer was five acres.

So Paul and Marjorie began their search, taking temperatures at different places in the mountains to determine the best place for the kind of grapes they wanted to make. Eventually they settled for their current parcel. Dave Bennion of Ridge and Bob Mullen of Woodside Vineyards advised them which varietal grapes thrived in the mountains, but the Staigers did all the hard work of putting in their grapes: Chardonnay, Cabernet Sauvignon and a small amount of Merlot. They built their winery and house, bonded their winery in 1973, and have been maintaining the vineyard and winery ever since.

The Staigers' vineyard is primarily dry-farmed, although garden hoses and buckets of water were dragged into the steep vineyard to nurture

- marine sandstone -- drains well, yet is dense enough to retain moisture.

Much of the northwest portion of the Santa Cruz Mountains AVA is affected by cold winds in May that come off the San Mateo coast. Even if these winds only lasted a day, they could upset the bloom, decreasing the size of their crop. The Staigers built a wind break of trees and regarded it as "just a question of meeting another of nature's challenges."

The Staigers are happy with what they do. "It forces you outside," Marjorie says. She admits that if she didn't have to care for the vineyard, she could be very lazy. They both find working with nature fun as well as challenging. "Nature never gives you the same cards to play with," Paul says.

Paul and Marjorie Staiger

Paul and Marjorie still maintain the entire vineyard themselves, except for laying out the bird netting and harvest. Paul has retired from the university, giving the couple's lives a more leisurely pace. They can take three months to cane prune the vines, and they only bottle one barrel at a time.

An aim of the Staigers is to make a wine that pairs well with food and lasts a long time. Since they do everything themselves, they feel they have no excuses for bad wine and are very careful about every step in the process. "Every bottle of wine is meant to be perfect," Paul says.

P•M Staiger

1300 Hopkins Gulch Rd.
Boulder Creek, CA 95006
Phone: (831) 338-4346
Web site:
www.pmstaiger.com
Annual Production: Under 400 cases
Winemaker: Paul Staiger
Winery Owners: Paul and Marjorie Staiger

Access
Open by appointment only

Tastings
No tasting fee
Wines: Chardonnay, Cabernet Sauvignon/Merlot blend

Sales of wine-related items? No

Picnics and Programs
Participates in Santa Cruz Mountains Winegrowers Association events

21850 Bear Creek Road
Los Gatos, CA 95033
Phone: (408) 354-1111
Web site:
www.byington.com/home.htm
Annual Production: 5000 to 6000
cases
Winemaker: Nick de Luca
Winery Owners: Bill and Mary
Byington

Access
Open daily 11-5

Tastings
No tasting fee
Private tours available for 10 or
more by appointment only
Wines: Chardonnay, Cabernet
Sauvignon, Gewurztraminer,
Marsanne, Pinot noir, Sauvignon
blanc, Viognier, Saignée, Alliage
blend (red), Liage blend (white)

Sales of wine-related items? Yes

Byington Wine Club
Two bottles every eight weeks at
about $50 each shipment;
Invitations to two annual events

Picnics and Programs
Picnic and barbecue area;
Event site for weddings, parties,
corporate events, winemaker
dinners and other events;
Participates in Santa Cruz
Mountains Winegrowers
Association events

Byington Vineyards and Winery

Far above the fog line at 2000 feet sits Byington Vineyards and Winery. The wine and the scenery bring you here. You bask in the sun with a bottle of wine, a picnic lunch and a friend. Up Wedding Hill behind the winery, you can stare across the peaks stretching to Bonny Doon and beyond to the Pacific Ocean. Life is good in the Santa Cruz Mountains.

Bill Byington, owner of Byington Vineyards and Winery, wants to share the lifestyle that wine making in the Santa Cruz Mountains brings -- good food, good wine and a relaxed environment.

Byington, owner of a steel heat treatment business (Byington Steel Treating) and former rancher, purchased the land on Bear Creek Road in the 1950s, but didn't start thinking about wine until his neighbor, David Bruce, wanted to lease the land to grow Pinot noir. Byington, an avid wine collector, decided that he'd rather make his own wine. In the 1980s, he got serious about the business, built the winery, planted the vines and created a destination worth the visit. The winery released its first wine in 1987. Byington recently expanded by purchasing 243 acres in the Paso Robles AVA to increase the winery's investment in Bordeaux-style wines, as well as to experiment with Rhône-style wines.

Bill Byington has assembled a team to make the dream of a "crown jewel" in the Santa Cruz Mountains a reality. Nick de Luca, the wine maker, works with cellar master Andrew Brenkwitz to create Chardonnay and red Bordeaux-style wines. De Luca went into the winery business straight from college in the early 1990s. He received his on-the-job training from many great winemakers in Sonoma County, including Paul Hobbs at Fisher Vineyards. He also spent two years in New Zealand, honing his skills at harvesting grapes under difficult conditions.

The design for Byington wines is to achieve a completely balanced flavor. Nick de Luca strives for a wine that is individual, complete and 100 percent genuine. According to de Luca, the winemaking is not formulaic; he does what is required to make a wine that is right. "We try not to believe our own voodoo," he says with a laugh.

Byington's Wedding Hill

Grapes are picked by taste, not by lab results, although sugar and acid measurements aren't ignored. The winemakers check the weather, the look of the vines and the fruit taste to determine when to pick.

The Chardonnay is made primarily from grapes in Los Carneros with an addition of grapes from three other vineyards in the Santa Cruz Mountains. The wine is barrel fermented *sur lees* for 10 to 11 months in French oak barrels. *Lees* are stirred bi-weekly to weekly.

Like many wineries in the Santa Cruz Mountains, Byington is looking to the Pinot noir grape as a good match for the area's shallow rocky soil and climate conditions, including its hot nights and even hotter days in the summer. The heat is balanced by a late spring (two months behind other areas) and an early, rapidly cooling fall. "It's almost a continental climate," de Luca notes, even though the winery is close to the water.

The nine acres surrounding the winery building are planted with Pinot noir. De Luca picks the grapes when they are "embarrassingly ripe," looking for a more tannic Pinot noir, with a dark fruit flavor and a baywood and pepper streak. He's increased the amount of whole clusters of grapes with stem inclusion during the fermentation to achieve this result.

The Cabernet Sauvignon grapes come from the mountain vineyards, primarily the Bates Ranch of the Santa Cruz Mountains. De Luca treats the Cabernet Sauvignon with a very Bordeaux approach. He ferments for 12 to 14 days, and leaves wine on the skins 30 to 60 days before barreling. He uses an increasing amount of American wood barrels because he believes American coopers are getting better at drying and toasting the barrels. A third to 50% of the barrels is new each year. The barrels are racked three to four times a year for aggressive aeration. The winemakers try for higher temperature fermentation (peak in mid-90° area) in the Cabernet Sauvignon to soften the tannins and give bigger, broader shoulders. De Luca has eliminated the use of commercial yeast, relying on naturally occurring yeast from the grapes. He feels that this method provides the wine with more of a feel of the vineyard from which it comes.

The Byington blend, Alliage, is based on a Bordeaux model, but the components vary each year as grape production and quality change. In 2002, de Luca leaned towards a heavier use of Cabernet Sauvignon, a moderate use of Cabernet Franc, and less use of Merlot, because he found that the Merlot grapes were not as good as they had been in previous years.

For full enjoyment, plan on spending time at the winery. Be careful as you approach the driveway because it's on a treacherous curve of the roadway. (Try not to be distracted by glimpses of the chateau-style winery through the grape vines.) Once you park, there's plenty of time to look around.

Start in the winery itself, a large room with a full length tasting bar, four to five wines to taste and gift and food items to browse. Recent

Saignée, Pinot noir and Cabernet Sauvignon. For Santa Cruz Mountains Winegrowers Association Passport holders, extra tastings are frequently available. These, as well as special winemaker dinners, are held in the caves. These caves were

three years in the making and among the first in the Santa Cruz Mountains. Enjoy the dark ambiance and the mystique of stacked barrels as you sip your wine or feast on a catered candlelit dinner.

Upstairs, check out the reception room and bridal room. Complete with fireplace, wet bar and full working kitchen, it is a well-lit, grand place for corporate events or wedding receptions. The surrounding balcony with views of the mountains and vineyard is also available for picnic lunches when events aren't in progress.

After you finish your tasting and your lunch, take a moment to walk up Wedding Hill. At the top of the red-brick path, you can enjoy the peace of the mountains, and, depending on the time of year, the roses that surround the small lawn.

As you leave the winery, remember that curve in the road and look closely before you pull out.

Byington Tasting Room

David Bruce Winery

21439 Bear Creek Rd.
Los Gatos, CA 95033
Phone: (800) 397-9972
            (408) 354-4214
Fax: (408) 395-5478
email:
DBW@davidbrucewinery.com
Web site:
www.davidbrucewinery.com
Annual Production: 60,000 cases
Winemakers: Tony Craig and
Michael Sones
Winery Owners: David and
Jeannette Bruce

Access
Open   weekdays 12-5;
            weekends 11-5

Tastings
No tasting fee; private tour and
tasting; $7.50 per person; private
cheese and fruit tasting $15.00
per person;
Wines: Chardonnay, Cabernet
Sauvignon, Grenache, Petite
Sirah, Pinot noir, Zinfandel

Sales of wine-related items? Yes

Private Cellar Club
20% discount on a case of wine
(requirement to be a member);
10% discount on non-wine items;
special events
Pinot Only Please option: three
bottles of select Pinot noir four
times a year at about $185 a
shipment

Picnics and Programs
Picnic area;
Event site for estate dinners and
corporate events;
Participates in Santa Cruz
Mountains Winegrowers
Association events

David Bruce Winery

David Bruce Winery is one of the older and more well-known wineries in the Santa Cruz Mountains. Founded in 1964, the David Bruce Winery is the realization of David Bruce's passion for winemaking. He's embraced a lifestyle that "many times says sacrifice," and acknowledges that "in order to get quality, you may need to give up quantity."

Bruce discovered wine in his long journey through medical school to become a dermatologist. He came from a teetotaler family, having his first beer only at the age of 19.

David's first venture with making wine had all the elements of a farce. Having heard from a buddy that his landlord had grapes that no one was picking and thinking he had permission, Bruce and his friends went to harvest their first grapes. Although things turned out fine, he didn't actually have permission and the fruit was Concord (table) grapes. Stomping grapes with their hands and feet, the students allowed the mixture to ferment in vats before pressing. Since they didn't have a grape press, they put the grapes between two boards on top of a plastic sheet. Then they rolled a car wheel back and forth to press the grapes, capturing the juice in the plastic sheet. According to David, it worked pretty well. Fermented and bottled, only about half the wine was drinkable, but Bruce was hooked nonetheless.

David bought 40 acres in the Santa Cruz Mountains in 1961, and planted vines on 25 of them. Then, the property contained German plum trees, the remains of a Christmas tree farm, a single frame house and barn, some shacks and some old, unidentifiable vines. Today, 16 of these acres at 2,200 feet (just above the fog line) contain Chardonnay, Pinot noir and Syrah grapes, as well as winemaking facilities.

Bruce was the initial winemaker, having worked at Ridge Winery in the late 1950s and early 1960s. He was very influenced by Martin Ray's style of clean, complex wines. Bruce was also a great experimenter, trying different methods to get the results that he wanted.

Some of his earliest wines were made without SO$_2$, in the style of Ray. However, that led to a slight problem in 1969. "I had some wonderful Pinot noir off the estate," Bruce recalls, "and in six months it went bad." He took the wine to UC Davis to find out what was wrong. They tested it and said the wine was fine. "They obviously hadn't tasted it," Bruce said. The wine had been contaminated by Brettanomyces yeast, which makes the wine taste a bit like wet dog's hair. However, the cause of the condition hadn't been identified in 1969. Once the culprit was found, it was determined that insuring correct amounts of SO$_2$ in the wine can reduce the chances of occurrence. Like many, but not all winemakers, Bruce adds the compound today to protect his wines.

David Bruce Vineyard

Since that time, David Bruce wines have won, and continue to win, multiple accolades. His Chardonnay was included in the 1976 blind tasting in Paris. Although the wine came in last, Bruce was proud to be included. His one clear vision, however, was "to make the greatest Pinot ever made." A firm believer that Pinot noir is the greatest grape, he dreams of a Pinot noir that has a velvety texture and a complex structure. Like others, Bruce believes that particular areas within the Santa Cruz Mountains within the area are ideally suited to the growth of Pinot noir.

In 1980 David Bruce decided to make the estate Pinot noir in the classic French method, clipping off whole clusters for the fermentation tanks and using "healthy individuals with big feet" to crush the grapes. His theory is that the human body is hard enough to crush the grapes, but soft enough not to pound the seeds, releasing too much tannin in the wine. The result brought him closer to the wine he wanted. The estate Pinot noir is still foot-crushed, although he has developed other mechanics (a pneumatic punch-down tool and a rotary fermenter) to simulate foot crushing.

For his non-estate wines, Bruce seeks to develop relationships with multiple vineyard owners. He looks for the "perfect vineyard" for each varietal grape. As a result, the winery obtains grapes from over 40 California winegrowers in more than 10 AVAs. Once the grapes are harvested, he feels his job is minimal. "Wine is made in the vineyard and the winery is the place where you make your wines worse" he says, and adds that the winemaker tries to "make them as little worse as possible."

David Bruce keeps different vineyard lots separate until final blending decisions are made. The best lots are bottled separately with vineyard designation, the rest are blended. Bruce doesn't believe that anyone has a "perfect palate." His team of winemakers makes the decisions about what to blend and what to leave alone. He wants David Bruce wines to have "mouth talk" and "come on" -- as in "come on for another bite to eat."

Bruce admits that the wine business is not the place to make a lot of ...

... the wine business beckons strongly and stays long enough, it becomes your life." The first moment he began to make wine he knew that it was a turning point in his life. "Sometimes," he says, "the change flits by on butterfly wings and people don't even notice it; other times it's as if a window opened up and people jump through it and kick themselves for ever after." Bruce continues, "Free will? I didn't have a bit of it. I *had* to do this."

David believes that there are three kinds of winemakers. The first includes those who really want to make a great wine; some accomplish the task and some go bankrupt in the pursuit. The second group includes people who understand finance and know how to manage people. These people create high visibility wines, but don't make the best wines per se. Then there is the person who wants to make himself a memorial. David Bruce looks around at the tasting room, event and office facilities and ruefully says, "I think I've built myself a memorial."

He also makes a good bottle of Pinot noir.

David Bruce

Zayante Vineyards

420 Old Mountain Road
Felton, CA 95018
Phone: (831) 335-7992
Fax: (831) 335-5770
email: info@
   zayantevineyards.com
Web site:
www.zayantevineyards.com
Annual Production: 2000 cases
Winemaker: Greg Nolten
Winery Owners: Greg Nolten,
Kathleen Starkey-Nolten, Marion
Nolten

Access
Open during annual open house
the weekend before Mother's
Day;
Otherwise open by appointment.

Tastings
No tasting fee
Wines: Chardonnay, Merlot,
Syrah, Zinfandel

Sales of wine-related items? Yes

Sampler Club
Two bottles four times a year that
will never exceed $50 a shipment

Picnics and Programs
Picnic area;
Participates in Santa Cruz
Mountain Winegrowers
Association events

A broad expanse of grape vines awaits you as you turn off narrow East Zayante Road. The sun is welcome after miles of dark redwood forests. You drive past the grape vines, park near the farmhouse that was destroyed in the 1989 Loma Prieta Earthquake and greet the Nolten's two Weimaraners, Gracie and Rita. Welcome to Zayante Vineyard's own bit of paradise.

The original vineyard, also called Zayante Vineyard, was planted in 1875 on a land grant signed by Ulysses S. Grant. Those vines were pulled up during Prohibition. Doc Mount purchased the property in the 1920s and put in an apple orchard. Land use changed once again during the 1950s as the apple trees were removed and cattle were allowed to graze. The sixth owners (husband and wife, Greg Nolten and Kathleen Starkey, and his parents, Bill and Marion) restored the land to its original use.

The Noltens bought the property in 1984 to satisfy a dream to have a vineyard. They planted the vines in 1988 and were bonded that year.

Marion and Greg Nolten

A family affair, Bill worked the fields during the day while Greg worked at a full-time job until Bill's death in 1996. Marion still helps Greg pour during tastings.

The family enjoys the hard work of a vineyard and winery, as well as the product. Greg and Kathleen, like many in the Santa Cruz Mountains, have a goal of sustainable agriculture. This is particularly important to them since they plan to pass their land and business to their two children, Andrew and Maggie. The Noltens are proud of the fact that their wines are made entirely from grapes grown on their property. "Everything is done on the estate," Kathleen says.

The south facing vineyard is planted with Chardonnay, Cabernet Sauvignon, Grenache, Merlot, Petite Sirah, Syrah and Zinfandel. While the vineyards are strictly organic, the Noltens have had to take extreme measures with the bane of California gardeners -- gophers.

Winemaker Greg Nolten didn't learn his trade in a formal way. He was the manager and wine buyer for the Cooper House Wine Cellar in Santa Cruz (destroyed by the 1989 earthquake). That's where, he says, he developed his palate. He also apprenticed in small vineyards in the mountains and was assistant winemaker at Sunrise Winery when it was on Empire Grade.

Like his approach with the vineyard, Greg believes in minimal interference with the wine. He takes the middle path with winemaking -- enough changes to make sure that the wines meet his expectations, but not so much that he manipulates the fruit into something else entirely.

Take the opportunity on a Passport Saturday to go up to Zayante Vineyard and stop for a picnic. Taste some of the hand-crafted estate wines, buy a bottle and sit down for lunch. You can gaze out over the vineyard and listen to the sounds of frogs, ducks and woodpeckers. When you're done, bask in the sun with a glass of wine and the sounds of chirpers and tweeters while you gaze at the untrellised vines.

A word of warning, though -- don't leave your picnic unattended. Gracie and Rita are waiting.

Generosa Winery

Generosa Winery

22630 Hutchinson Rd.
Los Gatos, CA 95033
Phone: (408) 286-1016
Fax: (408) 286-7390
email: info@generosa.com
Web site:
www.generosawinery.com
Annual Production: 1000 cases
Winemaker: Chris Gemignani
Winery Owners: Chris and Laura
Gemignani

Access
Open by appointment only

Tastings
No tasting fee
Wines: Super premium Tuscan-style wines made with Bordeaux and Italian varietal wines

Sales of wine-related items? No

Picnics and Programs
Participates in Santa Cruz Mountains Winegrowers Association events

When asked why he wants to make wine, Chris Gemignani offers a full explanation in a single sentence, "I come from an Italian family."

The family history is rich with winemaking, dating back to 18th century Italy. They brought their love of life and wine to San Francisco at the turn of the 20th century and, like many first generation immigrants, weren't particularly bothered by Prohibition. Chris's grandfather was a builder in San Francisco. One of his properties was a villa surrounded by a garden of bocce ball courts. Beneath the courts was a ten foot deep cellar filled with wine barrels. Every Sunday the hatch would be opened, Chris's Uncle Bruno would play the accordion, his grandmother would call the local *paesans* (Italian for countrymen) to invite them to the gathering, and Chris's mom would serve wine at five cents a glass. Chris reflects that those were real "days of heaven!"

Much of the Gemignani family still lives in Tuscany where winemaking is a way of life. During his college years Chris would visit *la familia* in Torre del Lago Puccini on the Tuscan coast, staying through the vineyard harvest. His *casetta* (small house) stood in the center of the vineyards with a cement fermentation tank on one side and cages of rabbits on the other. Through the years, Chris received a first-hand education in Italian-style winegrowing.

With this background, it was inevitable that Chris would make wine and in 1990, he started his home winemaking endeavor. Drawing on his heritage, he produces what he calls "California Super Tuscans." These rich and complex offerings are made with Bordeaux varietal wines blended with the Italian Sangiovese, Barbera, Charbono, Nebbiolo and Dolcetto wines. He goal is to create wine that is "*molto Italiano.*"

Chris believes that extraordinary richness and mouth-feel begins in the vineyard. To that end, he works closely with growers who will custom-farm their vineyard blocks to his specification. "Deficit water status after verasion and careful

to wine quality," he says. The attention to detail continues once the grapes arrive at the winery. "Every little berry has an impact," Chris says. To give an idea of their attention to detail, Chris and his wife, Laura, spent until two o'clock one morning washing cobwebs from Syrah grapes.

Laura and Chris Gemignani

At Generosa Winery, richness and mouth-feel are also enhanced in the cellar with such techniques as *cigne*. In this process some juice is taken away from the new must, thus deepening the wine's phenolic concentration. Some lots go through a triple *delestage*, a process of draining the fermentation tank of its juice, allowing the must to crush under its own weight, and then refilling the tank back with the now micro-oxygenated wine.

Chris ages the wine in French oak barrels for 18 to 24 months and further bottle-ages before releasing. The end result is a generous and rich *nettare di vino* (wine nectar).

The Gemignanis believe that food and wine are an inspiration to each other. As a result, many of their private tastings include delicious food pairings to be enjoyed in a setting with spectacular views of the Santa Cruz Mountains. The winery is named after Chris's late grandmother, Generosa. It's a fitting name for the wine and the people who make it: *generosa* means generous.

Burrell School Vineyards

24060 Summit Rd.
Los Gatos, CA 95033
Phone/Fax: (408) 353-6290
email: bsvine@earthlink.net
Web site:
www.burrellwine.com
Annual Production: 5000 cases
Winemaker: Dave Moulton
Winery Owners: Anne and Dave
Moulton

Access
Open Saturday and Sunday 11-5
  or by appointment

Tastings
$5.00 tasting fee, good towards
wine purchase
Tours available by appointment
only
Wines: Chardonnay, Cabernet
Franc, Merlot, Syrah, Zinfandel,
Valedictorian (Cabernet Franc,
Merlot and Cabernet Sauvignon
blend)

Sales of wine-related items? No

Winesipper's Club
Three bottles three times a year at
about $60 each shipment.

Picnics and Programs
Picnic area;
Event site for small weddings,
parties, winemaker dinners and
other events;.
Participates in Santa Cruz
Mountains Winegrowers
Association events

Burrell School Vineyards

"Welcome back to school," winemaker Dave Moulton says as he presents his wines. Gesturing towards the Chardonnay he continues, "You'll start in first grade and with graduation you'll get a diploma." He pushes a wine glass full of chocolates next to a bottle of Valedictorian. Obediently, you lift your glass of white wine as you stare at the well-tended vineyard and the view of the mountains beyond.

The view from the tasting room is far different from the one that Anne and Dave Moulton had in the mid-1960s. Then, they were living in East San Jose, and Dave was working as an engineer (a task he still performs) and brewing beer at home. One day, Anne stopped at the Mirassou winery down the road to pick up a bottle of wine. That single bottle of wine lured them into the world of wine volunteerism at their neighborhood winery. Soon Dave switched from home-brewed beer to home-made wine. During that time the Mirassou vineyards were falling victim to encroaching Silicon Valley, however, and Dave found himself picking grapes in competition with the bulldozers plowing under vineyards for the cultivation of new homes.

By the end of the 1960s, the Moultons decided it was time to own their own vineyard. In 1973 they purchased their land, ground that had been previously planted with grapevines by Lyman Burrell in 1854. Included with the purchase was a decrepit schoolhouse. (You can see a photo of the long-abandoned building in the tasting room.) They began to plant their vineyard. "We did everything wrong," Anne says. They planted the

The Burrell Schoolhouse

wrong vines for the area and their irrigation system failed. Out of a thousand planted vines, only two survived.

Discouraged, they turned their attention to the schoolhouse. They spent the next 20 years restoring it as their home.

By the time the 1989 Loma Prieta earthquake hit, Dave and Anne Moulton had owned their vineless vineyard for over 16 years. "That's when we decided to get serious," Dave says. Anne began planting vines, primarily Chardonnay. Since they'd learned from their earlier mistakes, these vines thrived.

At the same time, Dave began making wine seriously again. Since vines take from three to five years to create harvestable grapes, Dave had to obtain fruit from other people. "I was very selective about my grapes," he says, choosing to develop relationships with vineyard managers who carefully maintained their vines and land.

Burrell School Vineyard

Nearly a decade later, the Moultons are close to achieving their goal: sourcing all their wine grapes except Zinfandel from the Santa Cruz Mountains.

At an elevation of 1560 feet, the six-acre vineyard around the Burrell School winery is planted with Chardonnay, Merlot and Pinot noir. In 2001, Anne and Dave partnered with John McGinnis to purchase a 70-acre parcel (which they named the Pinchon Vineyard) in the Chaine D'Or portion of the Santa Cruz Mountains. Situated at an elevation of 1600 feet, the land has a long history of planted vines. It's from this vineyard that they are sourcing the remaining grape varieties that they use, including Merlot, Cabernet Franc, Cabernet Sauvignon and a small amount of Syrah. The only varietal grape they will continue to get from outside of the Santa Cruz Mountains will be Zinfandel.

Dave grew up in Iowa and understands the farming component of wine-making far too well. He's also the one responsible for maintaining the equipment needed for viticulture and wine-making. Of course, he notes, the equipment does have the tendency to break down at the worst possible moment. A born mechanic, Dave also has the ability to get the equipment up and running and will wax poetic about some of the aging farm machinery he uses.

Dave believes it's important to get the wine process going as quickly as possible when the fruit is ready. Picking, crushing, pressing and barreling for fermentation of Chardonnay are done within hours of each other. "We never wait," says Dave, "no matter when it's picked, even if it means we are working at one in the morning." With the exception of barreling, the same approach is true for Burrell School's red varietal wines.

There is an attention to detail in the development of Burrell School wines. Every nuance of the winemaking method (yeast, barrels, fermentation time, use of gravity rather than pumping, etc.) is designed to accentuate the fruit of the vine. Dave and Anne figure it will take 25-30 years of experimentation to get close to the perfection they hope to achieve. With the infinite colors you can put on the painting of the grape that becomes wine, Dave feels he would need to live another 400 years before he could create the perfect bottle of wine for his palate.

As you progress through your Burrell School education, take some time to look carefully at the tasting room, winery and gazebo. True to their interest in things old as well as new, the Moultons rescued wood from old buildings in the area. Some of the winery siding, the tasting room walls, as well as the gazebo in the picnic area come from Villa Bergstadt built in 1888. This retreat was the family home, doctor's office and summer retreat for San Francisco visitors of Dr. Goldmann, the villa owner. In its former location, the gazebo looked across a canyon to the Mare Vista Winery owned by Emile Meyer, a prominent Santa Cruz winery from the 1880s to the 1930s.

Burrell School is a small winery that has almost reached the capacity that the Moultons have planned. "We put our hands on everything," Dave says and they need to stay small to be able to maintain their hands-on approach and obtain the quality they desire.

So, drive up to the schoolhouse, start kindergarten all over again, and toast your graduation with the Valedictorian.

Dave Moulton pouring at the tasting room

Silver Mountain Vineyard

Silver Mountain Vineyard

Box 3636
Santa Cruz Mountains, CA 95063
Phone: (408) 353-2278
email: info@silvermtn.com
Web site:
www.silvermtn.com
Production:
Winemaker: Jerold O'Brien
Winery Owner: Jerold O'Brien

Access
Generally open the third Saturday
of the month; call for appointment.

Tastings
Tastings and tours available by
appointment
Wines: Chardonnay (Estate
Organic), Pinot noir, Zinfandel,
Alloy (Bordeaux blend)

Sales of wine-related items?
Limited

Top Flight
Four levels of club participation:
Two, four, six or twelve bottles per
shipment four times a year; prices
vary according to wines chosen

Picnics and Programs
Picnic facilities with view of
Monterey Bay; sunset and fireside
tastings;
Participates in Santa Cruz
Mountains Winegrowers
Association events

To be at Silver Mountain during Vintner's Festival is a pure joy. The 2,100 foot altitude of the vineyard gives you a clear view of surrounding mountains and the Monterey Bay. Jerold O'Brien pours wine in the tasting room. Art, music and good food, the ingredients of a great wine experience, are provided. You are glad you came.

A former Air Force fighter pilot, Jerold has been interested in the complexities and variations of wines since he was 22. While on the surface, winemaking may seem like a simple task, Jerold acknowledges that it is difficult to do well. There are so many variations in climate, grape growing and winemaking practices that it provides a challenge. And Jerold O'Brien is a man who loves a challenge.

Vintner's Festival at Silver Mountain

Zinfandel was the grape that brought Jerold to the vineyard. He found the Santa Cruz Mountains land in 1973 and bonded the winery in 1979. Around the same time, he planted ten acres of Mount Eden clone Chardonnay on his mountaintop vineyard. He has always used organic practices, and in 1991, the vineyard was certified organic.

Silver Mountain was the hardest hit winery in the 1989 earthquake. The quake caused a fire and the entire winery was destroyed. O'Brien thought long and hard about staying in the

business after that event. He acknowledges that it's difficult to make a living solely on the winery income. But the joy of the winemaker's life and pride in his product, as well as the challenge, led him to pick up the pieces and go on. It cost him two years, but in 1991, he was back in business. In the process of rebuilding he's added an amphitheater and entertainment facilities.

Jerold works closely with the vineyard owners and managers of his other sources of grapes. He says that trust is an important component in the relationship between a vintner and his grape grower, particularly if the grower is hours away. So, Jerold will take time to learn about the vineyard owner's farming practices before he establishes a permanent relationship with a grower. "It starts in the vineyard with the juice in the grapes," he says. "You buy the best you can obtain of premium quality grapes." He adds with a smile, "Then you have to be careful not to mess it up."

Santa Cruz Mountains grapes' are his first choice, because he believes the area produces the finest fruit in California. "We are the underdog," he says. "The mountain soil tends to be poor, without a lot of nutrients. As a result, the vines have to struggle to produce, which yields smaller lots of grapes with more character and complex flavors."

The same intensity of care goes into his winemaking. He uses two Old World practices, hand punch-downs and extended maceration, believing that these practices enrich the aroma and flavor of his wine.

It took Jerold O'Brien 21 years of experimentation to determine the ingredients of his Bordeaux blend, Alloy. He enjoys the blend better than any of its varietal components.

Jerold invites you to contact him and experience the unique Silver Mountain Vineyards. Once you have experienced the scenery and winery, Jerry hopes that you will relive that experience in every bottle of Silver Mountain wine that you enjoy.

Osocalis Distillery

Wending your way down a dirt path past chickens and a sheep, you come to a barn housing one of the two distilleries in the Santa Cruz Mountains. (The other is at Bonny Doon Vineyards.) Inside, an alambic still looking like a gigantic copper teapot at a mad tea party occupies a quarter of the building. Here Dan Farber, a very patient man, creates sumptuous distilled brandy, grappa and *eau de vie.*

Farber became "enamored with distillations" in the 1980s after spending many years making beer. When he moved to Santa Cruz in 1988 to attend graduate school, he decided he wanted to create brandy based on apples, and believed that the climate was well suited to producing quality fruit. He learned his craft by reading books, spending time in Cognac, France and at distilleries in California.

In 1994 he began to creating dry apple cider and apple brandies, only to find that a good market didn't exist for traditional ciders. Consequently, while he still makes a few cases of cider a year, Dan Farber has focused his efforts on producing apple and grape brandies.

While the process of brandy-making begins by making wine, the types of grapes used in production are different from those used in most California-made still wines. The two basic varietal grapes he uses are French Columbard and Pinot noir, but he also includes small amounts of varietal grapes such as Chenin blanc, Viognier and Carignan. Farber firmly believes in the process of blending in wines as well as brandies with the goal of a complex, well-constructed and elegant structure. "It's akin to putting together a perfume," he says.

The wine is processed through his alambic still, using heat to bring out the essence of the wine and, as a by-product, alcohol. The resulting liquid is placed into French oak barrels of various sizes, depending on the results that Farber is trying to achieve. The barrels have a very open grain and soft tannin structure giving the brandy a round smooth finish. The open grain causes a loss of three to four percent of the brandy per year -- "the angel's share." Once the liquid is barreled, the waiting begins. It takes an average of seven years before the brandy is ready to drink.

Farber's original still is an antique four-hectoliter alambic Charente built by Mareste, imported from the Charente region of France, and assembled by Farber. In 2003 he was able to obtain a 24-hectoliter Prulho still from the now-defunct Remy-Martin distillery in Carneros.

These brandies, like many California wines, tend to be more fruit forward and round in contrast to the elegant spiciness of French cognac. Farber tries to capture the *terroir* and climate of California in the bottle. He believes the taste should invoke the foggy oak covered vineyards and slow sunshine that lead to the intensity of fruit that he cultivates. The aging process concentrates and captures this essence.

Between a full-time job that requires frequent traveling, and waiting an average of seven years for the brandy to mature, Farber hasn't had much time for marketing or distribution. As a result, his brandy and hard cider can be difficult to obtain. But he doesn't see himself giving up his passion. "Once you catch the bug," he says, "it's all over."

Osocalis' Alambic Still

Osocalis Distillery

5579 Old San Jose Rd.
Soquel, CA 95073
Phone: (831) 477-1718
email: sales@osocalis.com
Web site: www.osocalis.com
Annual Production: 200 cases
Distiller: Dan Farber
Winery Owner: Dan Farber

Access
Open by appointment only

Tastings
No tasting fee
Alembic brandy, Norman style dry cider, grappa

Sales of wine-related items? No

Picnics and Programs
Participates in Santa Cruz Mountains Winegrowers Association events

Santa Cruz Mountain Vineyard

2300 Jarvis Rd.
Santa Cruz, CA 95065
Phone: (831) 426-6209
Web site:
www.scmvwine.com
Annual Production: About 2500 cases
Winemaker: Jeff Emery
Winery Owner (as of 2003; subject to change): Ken Burnap

Access
Open by appointment only

Tastings
No tasting fee
Wines: Cabernet Sauvignon, Duriff (Petite Sirah), Merlot, Pinot noir, Syrah, Bobcat Blend

Sales of wine-related items? No

Picnics and Programs
Participates in Santa Cruz Mountains Winegrowers Association events

Santa Cruz Mountain Vineyard

Tucked up a steep driveway at the end of Jarvis Road is a remnant of one of the oldest vineyards in the Santa Cruz Mountains, Santa Cruz Mountain Vineyard. It is also, according to owner and former winemaker Ken Burnap, the perfect place in California to make Burgundian Pinot noir.

In the 1970s, as co-owner of the Hobbit restaurant in Southern California, Ken traveled all over the state to find fine wines for the Hobbit, but was frustrated by the lack of what he considered good Pinot noir made in the Burgundian style. He decided there were two reasons why Californians couldn't make good Pinot noir. The first was the fickleness of the grape itself. "If it were a person, it would be committed," he says. The second was that people weren't planting Pinot noir under the optimum conditions.

Ken defined the 11 elements he felt were required to create the perfect place to grow Pinot noir grapes and proceeded to tell everyone what was wrong with where Pinot noir grapes were being grown. The frequent response was, "If you know so much, why don't you do it yourself?" Finally, David Bruce brought Ken to a piece of land that he was selling. Ken took soil samples, checked weather and compared the results to his criteria. It was, indeed, the perfect place to grow Pinot noir.

But Ken wasn't ready to buy. Instead, he picked up a bottle of champagne from a Santa Cruz liquor store and went back up to sit on the sunny hillside and say farewell to the perfect place. Within 15 minutes and a few sips, he'd changed his mind, and Santa Cruz Mountain Vineyard was born.

Over next three decades, Ken built his winery and added other varietal wines from purchased grapes to support his perfect Pinot noir. In 1979 he hired Jeff Emery, a student at UC Santa Cruz, for vineyard work and cellar help. By the time Emery graduated with a degree in geology, he was hopelessly seduced by the joys of growing grapes and making wine. "It's a field I will never have a total grasp and understanding of. One could view this as a frustrating liability, but I prefer to see it as a positive thing which keeps me pushing the limits of creativity and knowledge," Jeff says.

Burnap and Emery settled on methods that worked for them: picking the grapes based on taste and science, dry farming, hand cap punching for reds, aging in French oak for 12-18 months, fining and filtering when needed, wild yeast, addition of sulfur dioxide after fermentation when needed, and the like.

Jeff Emery

In July 2002 Ken Burnap decided to move in another direction. He remarried, put the winery up for sale and built a sailboat. He and his wife are sailing around the Mediterranean for the next few years, enjoying good food and wine.

The winery remains in the capable hands of Jeff Emery. "I feel very fortunate to be working in a job where there are different tasks to do at different times of the year," he says. He also enjoys the social aspect that is possible with a winery, finding that most of the customers are "interesting people who all have a certain common enjoyment of things that I consider important in life: good food, good conversation, a sense of adventure and the desire to cultivate meaningful connections between people.

Santa Cruz Mountains
Winegrowers Association

7605–A Old Dominion Ct.
Aptos, CA 95003
Phone: (831) 479-9463
Fax: (831) 688-6961
email: info@scmwa.com
Web site: www.scmwa.com

Santa Cruz Mountains Winegrowers Association

Santa Cruz Mountains Winegrowers Association

The Santa Cruz Mountains Winegrowers Association (SCMWA) is the core association for the Santa Cruz Mountains wineries. Because it was formed from two original organizations (Santa Cruz Mountain Vintners Association and the original Santa Cruz Mountains Winegrowers Association), it includes wineries that are in the Santa Cruz Mountains AVA, as well as those that aren't. The group decided that they wanted to have a inclusive membership rather than an exclusive one.

There are three levels of membership within the organization. General members own a commercial winery or distillery in Santa Cruz County or the Santa Cruz Mountains AVA. Special members are those who either produce wine commercially at a general member's facility or commercially produce wine from the Santa Cruz Mountains AVA outside the AVA boundaries. Associate members are those who have vineyards, wine related businesses or are interested in the Santa Cruz Mountains AVA.

It's a group drawn together for camaraderie, exchange of ideas and to provide a single voice for promotion of their viewpoint on wine, viticulture and winery issues. The winemakers provide recommendations and answers to each other, sell equipment and overages, and explore new ideas like sustainable agriculture. The association also puts on a trade show in a single location so that distributors don't have to travel all over the mountains to determine the wines they want to sell.

The association provides advantages for the wine consumers, as well. Four times a year, the association holds Passport Saturdays. Purchase of a "passport" gives you access to wineries that aren't normally open, or special tastings at those that are normally open. Passports can be obtained at association wineries or from the association itself.

The Vintner's Festival is a great annual event covering two weekends in June. Most of the wineries open either at their winery or set up at local restaurants. Good food is a welcome attendant at these venues. The entrance fee buys a souvenir glass for your tasting. Can't find a designated driver? Limousine companies can provide tours to the various locations during this festival.

An important benefit event is Wine with Heart. Held on a spring weekend, the dinner, tastings and auctions support the American Heart Association. The weekend is a great way to explore the Santa Cruz Mountains wineries at one venue, as well as support the community. Roman J. Bowser, Executive Vice President and CEO of the Western States Affiliate of the American Heart Association, says, "Wine with Heart has become a staple event for the American Heart Association, Santa Clara County. The funds raised by this event are directly invested into medical research, patient education and community outreach programs."

The number of wineries of the Santa Cruz Mountains is growing, and some of the older winemakers are moving on. Winemakers sometimes shift between the wineries or move in and out of the region. This book is a snapshot in time that gives you a place to start your exploration. Browsing the association web site, as well as those of individual wineries, gives you more information for your journey.

The spirit of the winemakers and winery owners in the mountains won't change, however. As history has shown, this is a stalwart group, surviving natural disasters and economic wars. And it's a group that works together to create the best wine in the mountain tradition.

The winemakers and winery owners embrace their jobs and their environment. They welcome you to their passion.

Passport Saturday - Page Mill Winery

Wine with Heart - Mary McLane and Roman J. Bowser of the
American Heart Association

Vintners Festival - River Run Vintners booth

Glossary

American Viticultural Area (AVA): A geographic area with similar climate, soil and environmental conditions whose boundaries are legalized by the Alcohol and Tobacco Tax and Trade Bureau (TTB).

appellation: Strictly speaking it refers to the French legal division of grape growing areas – *appellation controlee*. This division is the American Viticultural Area (AVA) in the United States. However, the word appellation is casually used as a substitution for an AVA.

bare root vine: A vine that has not been grafted on to a rootstock.

bench grafting (indoor grafting): Process of grafting a cutting (or clone) of a vine to a desired rootstock. The graft is kept indoors for about a year before being planted in the vineyard.

block: A section within a vineyard.

Brettanomyces (brett): A strain of yeast that can cause wine to acquire a taste that has been described as "wet dog hair." Injection of SO_2 during the winemaking process aids extreme cleanliness in avoiding this problem.

brix: A scale that measures sugar content in grapes.

bud wood: Vine grafted on to rootstock.

cap: Skins from red wine which float to the top during fermentation.

***Chaine D'Or* (golden chain)**: A phrase, probably coined by Paul Masson, that refers to the east side of the Santa Cruz Mountains from Woodside, to around Lexington Reservoir near Los Gatos. It was considered a premium grape growing region.

clone: A cutting from a grape vine that has the same genetic makeup as its parent vine.

clos: Fenced-in area enclosing a small vineyard.

custom crush: A facility that allows a winemaker without a winery to make wine on its premises.

district: A region within an appellation or AVA.

domaine: A Burgundian term for a collection of vineyard parcels owned by the same person.

fine: Clarify the wine by using agents such as egg whites or clays to absorb unwanted material.

maceration: Steeping crushed grapes with their skins.

malolactic (ML) fermentation: Transformation of malic acid into lactic acid. It's often done during red wine fermentation to soften the acidity of the wine.

MOG: Material other than grapes.

must: Unfermented or fermenting grape juice that is becoming wine.

native (wild) yeast: The natural yeast found on the grapes. This is different from commercial yeasts which some winemakers add to start the fermentation process.

phenolic compounds: Pigments and tannins in wine.

phylloxera vastatrix (phylloxera): A louse that attacks the roots of the vine. It devastated vineyards in Europe and America in the 1800s. Rootstocks were developed that are resistant to the louse.

Pierce's disease: A disease caused by a bacterium spread by insects, primarily the blue-green sharpshooter. It can devastate a vineyard. The correct plants around the vineyard can prevent the insects from getting to the vines.

prune: A way to shape the vine to insure the best possible fruit. There are several methods of pruning.

rootstock: Roots and bottom grape vine stem used as a basis for grafting clones. Biologists have developed rootstocks that are resistant to most diseases and insects that can affect grape vines.

***sur lees* (on the lees)**: A process of letting the lees, the insoluble material that drops out of wine, rest on the bottom of the tank or barrel during fermentation or aging. Some winemakers also stir the lees.

verasion: The moment when the grapes start to change color, about eight weeks after bloom.

vineyard designate: Wine made only with grapes from a particular vineyard.

vintage: The year the grapes for the wine were harvested and the winemaking process begun.

Further Reading

Books

Brook, Stephen, *The Wines of California*, Faber and Faber, New York, 1999.
Holland, Michael R., *Late Harvest, Wine History of the Santa Cruz Mountains*,
    The Late Harvest Project, Santa Cruz, CA. 1983.
Gleeson, Bill, *Backroad Wineries of California, A Discovery Tour of California's Country Wineries*,
    Chronicle Books, San Francisco, CA, 1989.
Jefford, Andrew, *Wine Tastes, Wine Styles*, Ryland Peters & Small, London, 2000.
Laube, James, *California Wine*, Wine Spectator Press, New York, 1999.
MacNeil, Karen, *The Wine Bible*, Workman Publishing, New York, 2001.
Margalit, Dr. Yair, *Winery Technology and Operations*,
    The Wine Appreciation Guild, San Francisco, CA, 1996.
Santa Cruz Sentinel, *5:04 P.M. The Great Quake of 1989*,
    Santa Cruz Sentinel Publishers Co., Santa Cruz, CA 1990.
Schaefer, Dennis, *Vintage Talk, Conversations with California's New Winemakers*,
    Capra Press, Santa Barbara, 1994.
Sullivan, Charles L., *Like Modern Edens, Winegrowing in the Santa Clara Valley and Santa Cruz Mountains 1798-1981*, California History Center, Cupertino, CA, 1982.
_____, *A Companion to California Wine*, University of California Press, Berkeley, CA, 1998.
Taber, Tom, *The Santa Cruz Mountains Trail Book*, Oak Valley Press, San Mateo, CA, 7th Edition, 1994.
Winkler, A.J., James A. Cook, W.M. Kliewer, Lloyd A. Lider, *General Viticulture*,
    University of California Press, Berkeley, CA,

Journals

Gibson, Ross Eric, "A History of Winemaking in the Santa Cruz Mountains,"
    San Jose Mercury News, June 29, 1993, p. 1B.

Pamphlets

Los Trancos Open Space Preserve, Mid-peninsula Regional Open Space District,   Los Altos, CA, 2001.
The Trail Center Peninsula Conservation Center,
    Peninsula Parklands, The Trail   Center, Palo Alto, CA, 2000.

Speeches

Ahlgren, Dexter, "A Brief History of the Santa Cruz Mountains Wines and Vines," July 24, 1988.

Web Sites:

pubs.usgs.gov/gip/earthq3
pugs.usgs.gov/publications/text/understanding.html
sepwww.stanford.edu/oldsep/joe/fault_images
www.scmwa.com

Winery Index

Ahlgren Vineyard, 92

Anderson Vineyard, 89

Aptos Vineyard, 80

Bargetto Winery, 74

Beauregard Vineyards, 65

Bonny Doon Vineyard, 62

Burrell School Vineyards, 102

Byington Vineyards and Winery, 96

Chaine D'Or Vineyards, 28

Cinnabar Vineyard and Winery, 52

Clos de la Tech, 33

Clos LaChance Wines, 54

Clos Tita Winery, 71

Cooper-Garrod Vineyards, 44

Cordon Creek , 88

Cronin Vineyards, 27

David Bruce Winery, 98

Equinox, 90

Fellom Ranch, 38

Fernwood Cellars, 57

Generosa, 101

Glenwood Oaks Winery, 72

Hallcrest Vineyards, 86

Hill Vineyards and Winery, 76

Kathryn Kennedy Winery, 46

Lonen and Jocelyn Wines, 47

McHenry Vineyard, 64

Michael Martella Wines, 32

Mt. Eden Vineyards, 43

Obester Winery, 60

Organic Wine Works, 86

Osocalis Distillery, 105

Page Mill Winery, 34

Pelican Ranch Winery, 66

Picchetti Winery, 36

P·M Staiger, 95

Ridge Vineyards, 40

River Run Vintners, 84

Salamandre Wine Cellars, 81

Santa Cruz Mountain Vineyards, 106

Savannah-Chanelle Vineyards, 50

Silver Mountain Vineyards, 104

Soquel Vineyards, 78

Storrs Winery, 68

Thomas Fogarty Winery and Vineyards, 30

Thunder Mountain Winery, 70

Troquato Vineyards, 48

Trout Gulch Vineyards, 82

Windy Oaks Estate Vineyards and Winery, 83

Woodside Vineyards, 26

Zayante Vineyard, 100

Tasting Notes

Tasting Notes

_____

_____

_____

_____

_____

_____

_____

_____

_____

_____

_____

_____

Tasting Notes

_____

_____

_____

_____

_____

_____

_____

_____

_____

_____

_____

_____

_____

Tasting Notes

Tasting Notes